COME TO MY
Tea Party

COME TO MY
Tea Party

*Whimsical teatimes
especially for children*

83 PRESS

Hoffman Media
1900 International Park Drive, Suite 50
Birmingham, Alabama 35243
hoffmanmedia.com

ISBN #978-0-9785489-7-1
Printed in China

ON THE COVER:
(Front Cover) From "Flutter by Butterfly,"
pages 43–59.
(Back Cover) Lemon-Coconut Scones from
"Teatime for Ballerinas," page 20.

Contents

Introduction

TEA PARTIES WITH DOLLS AND STUFFED ANIMALS ARE OFTEN A SPECIAL PART OF A CHILD'S FORMATIVE YEARS. But when those festivities instead involve favorite human friends, fanciful fare, warm beverages, and a truly special table setting, those tea parties become most memorable.

Children will squeal with delight for any of the eight whimsical teatime themes within these pages. From a dainty afternoon tea for ballerinas to a colorful fiesta for best amigos, there is something for all tastes and occasions. The food for each menu has been carefully crafted to reflect the primary motifs, such as in "Flutter by Butterfly," which begins on page 43 and is pictured on the cover. Tea wares and decorations follow suit, too, to make for a teatime that is also a feast for the eyes.

First-time hosts may find the concepts we present in "Tips for Hosting a Tea Party" (page 10) to be of great help. While our "Tea-Steeping Guide" (page 14) instructs on best practices for preparing a pot of delicious tea, the tea pairings for every menu have been expertly curated so that the infusions you serve are kid-friendly and work well with the fare as well as the theme. When possible, recipes include make-ahead tips for food preparation to minimize stress the day of the party as well as step-by-step photographs for more complicated techniques (page 124 and following). If you're concerned about entertaining guests who have gluten sensitivities, you will appreciate the index on page 135. This valuable reference highlights recipes that are completely gluten-free. We have also endeavored to include many recipes that are nut-free, so those with allergies will have good options.

Whatever the occasion, we hope you will be inspired to treat a dear child and his or her friends to a memorable and whimsical afternoon tea. Smiles will abound when they receive an invitation that says, "Come to my tea party!"

Tips for Hosting
A TEA PARTY

EXTENDING INVITATIONS

Formal invitations are a lovely and thoughtful way to communicate the details of the upcoming event, as well as to be sure you have an accurate count of those who will attend. Although invitations printed or written by hand and mailed are certainly preferred, technology has made it acceptable to extend them via telephone or email. However you choose to spread the word of your magical teatime celebration, plan early. Ideally, invitees should receive the communication a minimum of two weeks before the party. Invitations should include the following information:

- *Date and time of the event* (between 2:00 and 5:00 p.m., with 4:00 p.m. being preferred for afternoon tea, though an earlier time might be more suitable for children)

- *Address of venue*

- *Name of honoree(s)*

- *Name of host(s)*

- *Information and deadline for RSVP*

- *Preferred attire* (Specify only if clothing should be more formal or more casual than usual for a tea party or if costumes are encouraged to suit the theme.)

- *Gifts* (Specify only if gifts are not preferred or if they are to be given to a special cause, such as a charity.)

SELECTING AND SERVING HOT TEA

When choosing the types of tea to serve, offer a choice of at least two to accompany and complement your food selections. (The menus in this book feature a tea pairing for each of the courses.) Generally, strongly scented teas should be avoided unless they are favorites of the honoree. For children and caffeine-sensitive adult guests, opt for caffeine-free infusions, such as a fruity rooibos tea. For parents, grandparents, or other adults in attendance, serving classic blends, single-origin teas, or favorite fruit-flavored infusions would be a considerate gesture.

- *Use loose-leaf tea rather than prebagged. (See our "Tea-Steeping Guide" on page 14 for more information.)*

- *Make tea an hour or two ahead and keep it hot in insulated urns or thermal carafes in the kitchen until ready to serve. (Do not use containers that have ever held coffee, as the lingering oils from the coffee will impart an unpleasant taste to the tea.)*

- *In the kitchen, warm teapots with hot water, discard water, and fill teapots with hot tea from urns or carafes just before serving. (Let tea cool to a safe temperature before serving it to children, though.)*

- *During the party, filled teapots can be placed on tea warmers (stands outfitted with tea lights) away from the reach of children, if desired. Because it is not possible to regulate the heat they produce, resulting in scorched tea, tea warmers are not suitable for keeping tea hot for long periods. (To prevent burns, please make sure children are closely supervised.) Tea cozies are a safe alternative to tea warmers and are available in many pretty and practical designs.*

- *Select several adults to ensure that pots and cups remain full throughout the event. Having others assist with this task allows you ample time to give children your full attention while remaining a dutiful host. So your pourers can still enjoy the tea party, write down a set schedule in which each person serves for no longer than 20 minutes.*

PREPARING THE FOOD

Tea fare is usually best when made just before serving. Unless you have a lot of help in the kitchen, it is often logistically impossible to wait until the day of the event to prepare the food. Many of the recipes in this book include a "MAKE-AHEAD TIP" section, but general advice for making favorite teatime fare in advance follow.

- *Scones*—Freeze raw scones on parchment-lined baking sheets. Once frozen, transfer scones to airtight containers or bags, and store in the freezer for up to a month. Just before serving, place desired quantity of frozen scones (do not thaw) on parchment-lined baking sheets, and bake in a preheated oven according to recipe, allowing an additional 5 to 10 minutes for adequate doneness and browning, if necessary.
- *Tea Sandwiches*—Most fillings can be made a day ahead and stored in the refrigerator. Assemble sandwiches a few hours before the tea party, drape with damp paper towels, cover well with plastic wrap, and refrigerate until needed.
- *Sweets*—Most cakes, cupcakes, and cookies can be made at least a week in advance. Wrap cake layers tightly with plastic wrap, and place cookies in airtight containers with layers separated by wax paper. Store in the freezer for up to a week. Thaw completely before frosting or filling.

SETTING UP A BUFFET-STYLE TEA

The way you set up the food and tea can help avoid congestion when serving buffet style. If possible, arrange the plates, napkins, pastry forks, small knives, and food on one table, and place the teapots, cups and saucers, teaspoons, and any condiments for the hot tea (milk, sugar and/or honey, and lemon slices) on a sideboard or a wet bar. If beverages and food will be served from the same table, group the tea things on the right end of the surface so guests can serve themselves tea fare first and pick up the hot tea last.

- *When preparing food, planning for 2 or 3 of each item per adult guest and 1 or 2 per child can help prevent empty platters early into the party.*
- *Clearly designate a small table or other surface for used dishes.*

TEA-STEEPING *Guide*

The quality of the tea served at afternoon tea is as important as the food and the décor.
To be sure your infusion is successful every time, here are some basic guidelines to follow.

WATER

Always use the best water possible. If the water tastes good, so will your tea. Heat the water on the stove top or in an electric kettle to the desired temperature. A microwave oven is not recommended.

TEMPERATURE

Heating the water to the correct temperature is arguably one of the most important factors in making a pot of great tea. Pouring boiling water on green, white, or oolong tea leaves can result in a very unpleasant brew. Always refer to the tea purveyor's packaging for specific instructions, but in general, use 170° to 195° water for these delicate tea types. Reserve boiling (212°) water for black and puerh teas, as well as herbal and fruit tisanes.

TEAPOT

If the teapot you plan to use is delicate, warm it with hot tap water first to avert possible cracking. Discard this water before adding the tea leaves or tea bags.

TEA

Use the highest-quality tea you can afford, whether loose leaf or prepackaged in bags or sachets. Remember that these better teas can often be steeped more than once. When using loose-leaf tea, generally use 1 generous teaspoon of dry leaf per 8 ounces of water, and use an infuser basket. For a stronger infusion, add another teaspoonful or two of dry tea leaf.

TIME

As soon as the water reaches the correct temperature for the type of tea, pour it over the leaves or tea bag in the teapot, and cover the pot with a lid. Set a timer—usually 1 to 2 minutes for whites and oolongs; 2 to 3 minutes for greens; and 3 to 5 minutes for blacks, puerhs, and herbals. (Steeping tea longer than recommended can yield a bitter infusion.) When the timer goes off, remove the infuser basket or the tea bags from the teapot.

ENJOYMENT

For best flavor, serve the tea as soon as possible. Keep the beverage warm atop a lighted warmer or under your favorite tea cozy if necessary.

TEATIME FOR
Ballerinas

The
MENU

SCONE
Lemon-Coconut Scones
Organic Mango Strawberry Heaven

SAVORIES
Dressy Cucumber Canapés

Green Grape & Almond
Chicken Salad in
Parmesan Frico Cups

Pointe Shoe Tea Sandwiches
Organic Peach Rooibos

SWEETS
Vanilla Cupcakes with Pink
Almond–Cream Cheese Frosting

Strawberry Pointe Shoes

Blackberry Mini Pavlovas
Organic Lavender Rose

Tea Pairings by True Leaf Tea Company
346-701-7221 • trueleaftea.com

Delight aspiring prima ballerinas with a perfectly pink teatime in which each delectable course may be followed by a pirouette or a graceful curtsy.

Lemon-Coconut Scones

Makes 10

Luscious layers of a lemon curd–mascarpone cheese topping are piped atop flower-shaped, toasted-coconut scones to evoke the look of a tutu. Although no other condiments are really necessary, feel free to offer a fruity jam, such as raspberry, as well.

3 cups all-purpose flour
¼ cup granulated sugar
4 teaspoons baking powder
¾ teaspoon fine sea salt
½ cup cold unsalted butter, cubed
1 cup plus 2 tablespoons cold heavy whipping cream, divided
⅓ cup sweetened coconut flakes, toasted*
2 teaspoons fresh lemon zest
1 (8-ounce) container mascarpone cheese
¼ cup prepared lemon curd
Garnish: edible pink glitter

- Preheat oven to 375°. Line a rimmed baking sheet with parchment paper.
- In a large bowl, whisk together flour, sugar, baking powder, and salt. Using a pastry blender or 2 forks, cut butter into flour mixture until it resembles coarse crumbs. Using a fork, stir in 1 cup plus 1 tablespoon cream, toasted coconut, and lemon zest until a shaggy dough begins to come together. Working gently, bring mixture together with hands until a dough forms.
- Turn out dough onto a lightly floured surface, and knead gently until smooth by patting dough and folding it in half 4 to 5 times. Using a rolling pin, roll out dough to a ¾-inch thickness. Using a 2¾-inch flower-shaped cutter dipped in flour, cut as many scones as possible from dough without twisting cutter, rerolling scraps once. Place scones, evenly spaced, on prepared baking sheet. Freeze scones for 10 minutes.
- Brush tops of scones with remaining 1 tablespoon cream.
- Bake until golden brown, 16 to 20 minutes. Let cool completely.
- In a small bowl, beat together mascarpone cheese and lemon curd with a mixer at medium speed until smooth. Transfer mixture to a piping bag fitted with a small petal tip (Wilton #104). Working with one scone at a time and beginning on outer edge of each scone, pipe mixture in concentric, overlapping, ruffled circles on top of scone to resemble the layers of a tutu.
- Garnish scones with edible pink glitter, if desired.

*To toast coconut, preheat oven to 300°. Place coconut in a single layer on a parchment-lined rimmed baking sheet. Bake until golden brown, checking every 5 minutes and stirring occasionally. Let cool completely before using.

RECOMMENDED CONDIMENT:
Seedless raspberry jam

"Ballet is like a rose. It is beautiful and you admire it, but you don't ask what it means."

—GEORGE BALANCHINE

Dressy Cucumber Canapés
Makes 12

Cucumber tea sandwiches are classic choices for afternoon tea, and these cream-cheese iterations of the popular savory are perfect for a ballet-themed event.

1 English cucumber
12 wide slices whole-wheat sandwich bread, frozen
¾ cup cream cheese, softened
1½ teaspoon fresh lemon zest
¾ teaspoon fresh lemon juice
¾ teaspoon kosher salt
Garnish: fresh lemon zest

• Using a fork, scrape sides of cucumber lengthwise to create lines. Using a sharp knife or a mandoline, slice cucumber into 42 (1⁄16-inch-thick) rounds. Cut each round in half. Place cucumber halves on paper towels to absorb liquid.
• Using a 4-inch ballerina tutu–shaped cutter*, cut 12 shapes frozen bread, discarding scraps. To prevent bread from drying out, cover with damp paper towels or place in a resealable plastic bag, and let thaw at room temperature.
• In a small bowl, stir together cream cheese, lemon zest, lemon juice, and salt until smooth and well combined.
• Referring to how-to photographs on page 124, spread a thin, even layer of cream cheese mixture onto each bread shape. Shingle 7 cucumber pieces over tutu area of bread shapes. Transfer remaining cream cheese mixture into a piping bag fitted with a small French star tip (Wilton #28) and pipe a "belt" just above shingled cucumbers. Serve immediately, or cover with damp paper towels, place in a single layer in a covered container, and refrigerate for a few hours until ready to serve.
• Just before serving, garnish each canapé with lemon zest along neckline area of leotard, if desired.

We used an Ann Clark cookie cutter, available from amazon.com.

Green Grape & Almond Chicken Salad in Parmesan Frico Cups

Makes 24

Bits of chopped celery and toasted almonds provide welcome crunch to this chicken salad that gets its sweetness from green grapes. Although it is certainly tasty as a sandwich filling, rounded scoops of the salad look oh-so pretty served in ruffled and dainty Parmesan Frico Cups.

1½ cups chopped roasted chicken breast*
½ cup chopped green grapes
6 tablespoons mayonnaise
2½ tablespoons chopped toasted slivered almonds
2 tablespoons chopped celery
½ teaspoon dried tarragon
⅛ teaspoon ground black pepper
Parmesan Frico Cups (recipe follows)
Garnish: thinly sliced green grapes

• In a large bowl, stir together chicken, chopped grapes, mayonnaise, almonds, celery, tarragon, and pepper.

Cover, and refrigerate for 4 hours to let flavors meld.
• Just before serving, divide chicken salad among Parmesan Frico Cups.
• Garnish with sliced grapes, if desired. Serve immediately.

*We used white meat from a rotisserie chicken.

Parmesan Frico Cups

Makes 24

Melted circles of Parmesan cheese become lovely lacy, edible cups when draped while warm over the backs of the wells of a miniature muffin pan. For best color and texture, it is important to grate cheese from a wedge instead of purchasing pre-grated cheese.

1½ cups freshly coarsely grated Parmesan cheese*

• Preheat oven to 350°. Line 4 rimmed baking sheets with parchment paper.
• Working in batches and with one prepared baking

sheet at a time, arrange 6 (1-tablespoon) mounds cheese into 2½-inch circles, 2 inches apart.
• Bake until cheese is melted and bubbly, 6 to 8 minutes. Remove from oven, and let stand for 30 seconds. Working quickly and using a thin-edge spatula, lift cheese wafers, and drape over wells of an inverted mini muffin pan. Let cool completely. Repeat with remaining cheese. Store in an airtight container until needed, and use within 24 hours.

We used the largest hole of a box-style grater.

Pointe Shoe Tea Sandwiches
Makes 12

Ham and cheese get a fruity boost from raspberry preserves spread on the inside of these charming tea sandwiches and piped on the outside as ribbons for our pointe shoe ham garnishes.

24 very thin slices white sandwich bread, frozen
12 slices Muenster cheese
24 thin slices deli ham
¼ cup seedless raspberry preserves

• Using a 4¼-inch pointe shoe–shaped cutter*, cut 24 shapes from frozen bread, discarding scraps. To prevent bread from drying out, cover with damp paper towels or place in a resealable plastic bag, and let thaw at room temperature.
• Using the same cutter, cut 12 shapes from cheese and 24 shapes from ham, discarding scraps.
• Spread a thin layer of raspberry preserves onto 12 bread shapes. Top each with a cheese shape and a ham shape. Cover each with a remaining bread shape.
• Referring to how-to photographs on page 125 and using a paring knife, cut remaining 12 ham shapes to fit onto the "shoe" portion of the sandwiches, and place a ham shape on top of each stack. Serve immediately, or cover with damp paper towels, place in a single layer in a covered container, and refrigerate for a few hours until ready to serve.
• Just before serving, place remaining raspberry preserves in a small piping bag and cut a ¼-inch hole in tip. Pipe crisscrossing lines onto exposed bread at top of sandwich to create the ribbons of a pointe shoe. Serve immediately.

We used Ann Clark cookie cutters, available from amazon.com.

Vanilla Cupcakes with Pink Almond–Cream Cheese Frosting

Makes 48

Cake flour provides a pleasing soft texture for these vanilla-flavored cupcakes, which serve as the perfect canvas for a decadent cream cheese frosting that is laced with more vanilla and a bit of almond extract and garnished with a dusting of sparkling sugar.

½ cup unsalted butter, softened
1 cup granulated sugar
2 large eggs, room temperature
1½ cups unbleached cake flour
1½ teaspoons baking powder
¼ teaspoon fine sea salt
½ cup whole milk, room temperature
½ teaspoon vanilla extract
Pink Almond–Cream Cheese Frosting (recipe follows)
Garnish: pink sparkling sugar

• Preheat oven to 350°. Line a 48-well mini muffin pan with paper liners.
• In a large bowl, beat together butter and sugar with a mixer at medium speed until light and fluffy, approximately 3 minutes. Add eggs, one at a time, beating after each addition until incorporated.
• In a medium bowl, whisk together flour, baking powder, and salt. Add to butter mixture, alternately with milk and vanilla, in thirds, beginning and ending with flour mixture, beating at low speed until combined. Using a 2-teaspoon levered scoop, divide batter among wells of prepared pan. (There might be batter left over.) Tap pan on countertop several times to level batter.
• Bake until a wooden pick inserted in centers comes out clean, 9 to 11 minutes. Let cool completely on wire racks.
• Place Pink Almond–Cream Cheese Frosting in a piping bag fitted with a large French star tip (Ateco #869). Pipe an upright dollop of frosting on the top of each cupcake.
• Garnish with pink sparkling sugar, if desired. Serve immediately, or store cupcakes in an airtight container, and refrigerate for up to 3 days.

Pink Almond–Cream Cheese Frosting

Makes approximately 3½ cups

Cream cheese and butter are the base for this luscious topping. Flavor it with the extracts indicated, or substitute to taste with other ones, such as strawberry or lemon.

7 cups confectioners' sugar
1 (8-ounce) package cream cheese, at room temperature
½ cup unsalted butter, softened
½ teaspoon almond extract
¼ teaspoon vanilla extract
¼ teaspoon kosher salt
3 tablespoons whole milk
Pink gel food coloring

• In a large mixing bowl, beat together confectioners' sugar, cream cheese, butter, extracts, salt, and milk at low speed with a mixer. Beat in enough pink food coloring to achieve desired color. Increase speed to high, beating until light and fluffy. Use immediately, or transfer to an airtight container, and refrigerate for up to a day. Let come to room temperature, and beat with a mixer for 1 minute before using.

Strawberry Pointe Shoes

Makes 12

Fresh strawberries will look quite fancy when decked out with a coating of vanilla-flavored melting wafers in two colors to resemble pointe shoes.

1½ cups white vanilla-flavored melting wafers*
12 large fresh strawberries
Pink icing food coloring

• Line a rimmed baking sheet with parchment paper.
• In a small microwave-safe bowl, microwave melting wafers in 30 second intervals until completely melted, stirring between each interval.
• Wash strawberries and pat completely dry with a paper towel.
• Referring to how-to photographs on page 126, dip each strawberry into melted wafers, leaving a small amount of strawberry showing at the top. Place dipped strawberries on prepared baking sheet and let set at room temperature, approximately 10 minutes.

• If melted wafers in bowl have solidified any, rewarm in microwave oven in 10-second intervals. Add pink food coloring to melted wafers in bowl until desired color is achieved. Carefully dip sides of strawberries in pink mixture, leaving a triangle of white exposed in center of each strawberry. Return strawberries to prepared baking sheet and let set at room temperature, approximately 10 minutes.

• Transfer remaining pink mixture to a small piping bag and cut a ⅛-inch hole in tip. Pipe crisscrossing lines over the exposed white area, connecting the 2 pink sides and creating the ribbons of a pointe shoe. Refrigerate until ready to serve.

*We used Ghirardelli.

Blackberry Mini Pavlovas

Makes 10

Anna Pavlova is the world-famous Russian ballerina of the 1920s for whom this meringue dessert is named. Often attributed to an Australian chef, the sweet treat is typically filled with whipped cream and fruit (usually passionfruit in Australia, but kiwi in New Zealand). Our petite version show-cases blackberries two ways—as preserves spread into the bottom of the meringue shells and as a fresh berry garnish.

3 egg whites, room temperature
¼ teaspoon cream of tartar
¼ teaspoon kosher salt
1 cup castor sugar*
¼ teaspoon vanilla extract
⅔ cup blackberry preserves
Sweetened Whipped Cream (recipe follows)
30 small fresh blackberries or 15 large fresh
   blackberries, halved

• Position oven rack in center of oven. Preheat oven to 300°. Line a rimmed baking sheet with parchment paper. Referring to how-to photographs on page 127 and using a pencil, draw 10 (2-inch) circles onto parchment paper; turn parchment over.

• In the bowl of a stand mixer fitted with the whisk attachment, beat together egg whites, cream of tartar, and salt at medium-low speed until soft peaks form, 5 to 6 minutes. With mixer on low speed, add sugar in a slow, steady stream, beating until combined. (This should take approximately 3 minutes.) Increase mixer speed to medium, and beat until thick and shiny, 10 to 12 minutes, stopping to scrape down sides of bowl halfway through. Rub meringue between 2 fingers to make sure it is smooth, and no sugar granules can be felt. Beat in vanilla extract at medium-high speed until combined, approximately 30 seconds. Transfer meringue mixture to a piping bag fitted with a medium open-star tip (Ateco #826).
• Starting in the center of each circle, pipe concentric circles of meringue outward until each drawn circle is filled. Pipe 1 to 2 extra layers onto perimeters to form a rim around the edge of each circle. Place meringues in oven.
• Immediately reduce oven temperature to 225°. Bake until dry and firm to the touch, 45 minutes to 1 hour. Turn oven off and leave meringues in oven with door closed for at least 8 hours. Store until needed at room temperature in an airtight container with layers separated with wax paper.
• Just before serving, spread a scant 1 tablespoon blackberry preserves into each meringue. Fill meringues with Sweetened Whipped Cream. Top each with 3 small blackberries or 3 large blackberry halves.

*To make castor sugar, place granulated sugar in the work bowl of a food processor, the container of a blender, or a spice grinder. (If using a large food processor, make sure there is enough sugar to cover the blades.) Pulse a few times until sugar resembles fine sand. (Make sure you don't pulse too much; otherwise, you'll end up with confectioners' sugar.)

Sweetened Whipped Cream

Makes approximately 1 cup

By whisking together cold heavy cream and sugar, you quickly get a tasty topping or filling for desserts or scones. Because the amounts of the ingredients are rather small, we recommend doing the whisking by hand instead of with a mixer.

½ cup cold heavy whipping cream
¼ cup granulated sugar

• In a large bowl, whisk together cream and sugar until medium-stiff peaks form. Use immediately, or refrigerate for a few hours until ready to use.

UNDER THE

Big Top

The
MENU

SCONE
Golden Raisin & Oat Scones

Banana Muffin Herbal Tea

SAVORIES
Chicken Nugget Lollipops
with Mayo Ketchup

Clown Canapés

Pizza—Mac & Cheese Swirls

Razzmatazz Herbal Tea

SWEETS
Mini Caramel Apple Cupcakes

Chocolate Pudding
with Vanilla Whipped Cream

Kettle Corn Fun Mix

Blueberry Boost Herbal Tea

Tea Pairings by The Boulder Tea Company
303-817-7057 • boulderteaco.com

Bring the magic of the
"greatest show on earth"
to your table with colorful
wares and exciting,
circus-inspired treats.

1/3 cup firmly packed light brown sugar

1 tablespoon baking powder

1/2 teaspoon fine sea salt

6 tablespoons cold unsalted butter, cubed

1/3 cup golden raisins, chopped

1/2 cup plus 1 tablespoon cold heavy whipping cream, divided

1 large egg

1/2 teaspoon vanilla extract

Garnish: chocolate-hazelnut spread**

• Preheat oven to 400°. Line a rimmed baking sheet with parchment paper.

• In a large bowl, whisk together flours, oats, brown sugar, baking powder, and salt. Using a pastry blender or 2 forks, cut butter into flour mixture until it resembles coarse crumbs. Stir in raisins.

• In a liquid-measuring cup, whisk together 1/2 cup cream, egg, and vanilla extract. Add to flour mixture, stirring just until ingredients are combined and a shaggy dough begins to form. Working gently, bring mixture together with hands until a dough forms. (Dough will be firm once it comes together.)

• Turn dough out onto a lightly floured surface, and knead gently until smooth by patting dough and folding it in half 4 to 5 times. Divide dough into 2 equal portions. Using a rolling pin, roll out each portion of dough to a 3/4-inch-thick round. (Each portion should measure approximately 5 inches in diameter.) Pat edges of dough rounds to neaten and smooth. (If dough has warmed and seems soft, freeze for 10 minutes.) Using a long sharp knife, cut each portion into 6 equal wedges. Place scones 2 inches apart on prepared baking sheet.

• Brush tops of scones with remaining 1 tablespoon cream.

• Bake until edges of scones are golden brown and a wooden pick inserted in centers come out clean, approximately 12 minutes. Let cool completely.

• If desired, place chocolate-hazelnut spread in a piping bag and cut a small hole in tip of bag. Pipe a squiggle of chocolate-hazelnut spread to garnish cooled scones. Serve within a few hours.

*Spoon flour into measuring cup without packing and then scrape off excess with a straight edge to level.

**We used Nutella.

RECOMMENDED CONDIMENT:

Seedless strawberry jam

Golden Raisin & Oat Scones

Makes 12

Toothsome, wedge-shaped scones are laden with sweet bits of golden raisin juxtaposed with the nutty and earthy notes of oats and whole-wheat flour. For a really decadent treat, drizzle with chocolate-hazelnut spread and serve with a favorite jam on the side.

1 cup whole-wheat flour*

1/2 cup all-purpose flour*

1/2 cup quick-cooking oats

Chicken Nugget Lollipops

Makes 24

Most children really like to eat chicken nuggets, and these whimsical, made-from-scratch iterations that mimic lollipops are sure to be a hit, especially when served with a tasty dipping sauce.

6 large frozen ice-glazed chicken tenderloins*, thawed
2 cups whole milk
4 cups cornflakes cereal
½ teaspoon fine sea salt
⅛ teaspoon ground black pepper
24 sour cream and onion–flavored twisted pretzel
    sticks**
Garnish: 24 fresh chives
Mayo Ketchup (recipe follows)

• Preheat oven to 375°. Line a rimmed baking sheet with foil. Spray foil with cooking spray.
• Cut each chicken tenderloin into 4 equal-size nuggets.
• In a medium bowl, combine milk and chicken. Let chicken soak in milk for 15 minutes.
• Place cereal in a large resealable plastic bag. Using a rolling pin, coarsely crush cereal. Add salt and pepper to bag and shake until well combined. Transfer cereal mixture to a pie plate or a wide shallow bowl.
• Drain chicken, discarding milk. Place each chicken nugget in cereal mixture, coating all sides of chicken nuggets and pressing firmly to adhere coating. Place coated nuggets on prepared baking sheet.
• Bake until chicken meat is white and opaque and an instant-read meat thermometer reaches 170° when inserted into thickest portion, 20 to 25 minutes, turning nuggets over halfway through cooking time for even browning. Let chicken cool slightly.
• Using a sharp paring knife or kitchen scissors, cut a small slit into the end of each chicken nugget. Insert a pretzel stick firmly into each slit.
• Tie each pretzel stick with a fresh chive for garnish, if desired. Serve immediately with Mayo Ketchup for dipping.

*For best texture, it is important to use chicken tenderloins that are frozen with a 15% chicken broth solution, such as Tyson, for this recipe.
**We used Snyder's of Hanover's.

Mayo Ketchup

Makes 1 cup

A simple mixture of equal parts mayonnaise and ketchup is enhanced with freshly squeezed lemon juice and a touch of garlic powder in this easy dipping sauce. Be sure to make it several hours ahead so flavors have a chance to meld.

½ cup mayonnaise
½ cup ketchup
2 teaspoons fresh lemon juice
¼ teaspoon garlic powder

• In a small bowl, stir together mayonnaise, ketchup, lemon juice, and garlic powder. Cover and refrigerate for flavors to meld, up to a day in advance.

Clown Canapés

Makes 12

These whimsical savory bites are cheery and not scary, and they're gluten-free to boot.

1 (8-ounce) package cream cheese, softened
12 small round rice crackers
1½ teaspoons everything bagel seasoning blend
12 bugle-shaped corn snacks
12 cherry tomatoes
1 medium carrot, peeled

• Referring to how-to photographs on page 128, place cream cheese in a piping bag fitted with a large open star tip (Wilton #1M). With tip perpendicular to cracker, pipe a ruffled dollop of cream cheese onto each cracker. Sprinkle with seasoning blend. Place a tomato onto cream cheese on each cracker, blossom end down, pressing down slightly to adhere. Pipe another cream cheese dollop onto top of each tomato. Top with a corn snack, pressing down slightly to adhere.
• Finely grate enough carrot to resemble frizzled clown hair. Arrange grated carrot as desired on cream cheese at base of corn snacks. Cut a few (⅛-inch-thick) crosswise slices from remaining carrot. Using a small round piping tip (Wilton #10) as a cutter, cut 12 circles from carrot slices. Using a small amount of cream cheese, adhere carrot circles to tomatoes for noses. Serve immediately, or refrigerate for up to an hour before serving.

Pizza–Mac & Cheese Swirls

Makes 24

A mashup of two childhood comfort foods, these colorful rollups, whether served warm or at room temperature, are sure to be a hit with partygoers.

2 cups cooked elbow macaroni, warm
1 cup shredded mozzarella cheese
½ cup shredded Colby cheese
¼ cup coarsely grated Parmesan cheese
2 tablespoons heavy whipping cream
1 tablespoon salted butter, melted
2 (8-inch) flour tortillas*
2 (8-inch) spinach herb tortillas*
¼ cup prepared pizza sauce, divided
12 very thin slices sandwich pepperoni**
12 very thin slices capicola ham
12 very thin slices genoa salami

• In a medium bowl, stir together warm macaroni, cheeses, cream, and butter until well combined. Transfer mixture to a rimmed baking sheet, and pat approximately 1-inch thick into an even 7x6-inch rectangle. Cover and refrigerate until firm. When macaroni mixture is cold and will hold together, cut into 4 (7x1½-inch-wide) logs.
• Place tortillas in a single layer on a work surface. Spread each tortilla with 1 tablespoon pizza sauce, leaving a 1-inch border around edges. On each tortilla, place 3 salami slices on top of pizza sauce, overlapping meat to cover sauce. Top salami with 3 ham slices and then 3 pepperoni slices. Place a cold macaroni log on bottom edge of each tortilla. Roll up each tortilla firmly to encase ingredients, ending with seam side down. Wrap securely in plastic wrap and refrigerate until needed, up to a day. When ready to serve, unwrap and place on a cutting surface. Using a serrated bread knife in a gentle sawing motion, trim and discard at least 1 inch from each end of tortilla rolls, and cut each tortilla roll into 6 slices. Serve at room temperature or warm. To serve warm, place slices on a microwave-safe plate and heat on high in 15-second intervals until centers are warm. Serve immediately.

*We used Mission.
**Sandwich pepperoni is available in the deli and is larger than pre-sliced pepperoni.

GLUTEN-FREE OPTION: *Replace the macaroni and tortillas with gluten-free versions, and make sure all meats are certified gluten-free.*

Mini Caramel Apple Cupcakes
Makes 64

These dainty cupcakes topped with dulce de leche and chopped apple evoke memories of eating caramel-covered apples at the circus.

¾ cup unsalted butter, softened
1½ cups granulated sugar
¼ teaspoon fine sea salt
3 large eggs, room temperature
¾ teaspoon vanilla extract
1½ cups sifted cake flour
½ cup heavy whipping cream
2 (13.4-ounce) cans dulce de leche
1½ cups finely chopped red apple with peel

• Preheat oven to 325°. Line 64 wells of several mini muffin pans with baking cups.
• In a large bowl, beat together butter, sugar, and salt at medium speed with a mixer until light and fluffy, approximately 3 minutes. Scrape down bowl. Beat in eggs, one at a time. Beat in vanilla extract. Add flour, alternating with cream in three additions, beginning and ending with flour, scraping down bowl as necessary.
• Using a 2-teaspoon levered scoop, drop batter into bake cups. (Don't overfill, or bake cups will overflow.) Tap pan gently on countertop to level batter.
• Bake just until a wooden pick inserted in centers comes out clean, 11 to 13 minutes. (Don't overbake, or cupcakes will be dry.) Remove cupcakes to a wire cooling rack and let cool completely.
• Place dulce de leche in a piping bag fitted with a large open star tip (Wilton #1M). Pipe a decorative swirl on top of each cupcake.
• Just before serving, garnish each cupcake with chopped apple.

Chocolate Pudding with Vanilla Whipped Cream

Makes 6 (⅓-cup) servings

Kids of all ages are sure to enjoy this luscious, homemade chocolate pudding, which is thickened with cornstarch, especially when each serving is topped with vanilla-flavored whipped cream and garnished with colorful sprinkles.

½ cup granulated sugar
¼ cup unsweetened cocoa powder
2 tablespoons cornstarch
¼ teaspoon fine sea salt
2 cups whole milk
1 tablespoon unsalted butter
1 teaspoon vanilla extract
Vanilla Whipped Cream (recipe follows)
Garnish: rainbow sprinkles

• In a medium saucepan, whisk together sugar, cocoa powder, cornstarch, and salt. Gradually whisk in milk, a small amount at a time, until mixture is fairly smooth.
• Bring mixture to a low boil (a few bubbles breaking the surface) over medium heat, stirring constantly. Cook, stirring constantly, until pudding thickens, 2 to

3 minutes. Remove pan from heat, and add butter and vanilla extract, stirring until butter melts. Divide pudding among 6 heatproof dessert dishes. Cover surface of pudding with plastic wrap and refrigerate until completely cold, several hours and up to a day, before serving.
• Just before serving, place Vanilla Whipped Cream in a piping bag fitted with a large open star tip Wilton #1M. Pipe a large dollop of cream on top of cold pudding.
• Garnish with rainbow sprinkles, if desired.

Vanilla Whipped Cream

Makes 2 cups

Three ingredients are all that are needed for this delicious topping. Be sure that the heavy cream is cold so it will whip to the correct volume and consistency.

1 cup cold heavy whipping cream
2 tablespoons confectioners' sugar
½ teaspoon vanilla extract

• In a deep bowl, beat together cream, confectioners' sugar, and vanilla extract at high speed with a mixer until thickened and soft peaks form. Use immediately.

Kettle Corn Fun Mix

Makes 12 cups

Perfect for party favors, this fun mixture of animal crackers, candies, cereal, and more will delight the eyes and the taste buds. Homemade kettle corn is the base for this treat, but if time is short, skip the corn popping and use 8 cups of store-bought kettle corn instead.

2 tablespoons extra-virgin olive oil
¼ cup popcorn kernels, divided
2 tablespoons granulated sugar
½ teaspoon fine sea salt
2 cups animal crackers
2 cups fruit-flavored corn cereal
1 cup multicolored fruit-flavored jelly beans
1 cup mini chocolate-covered chocolate candies

• In a very large saucepan covered with lid, heat oil on medium-high heat with 3 popcorn kernels. When kernels pop, add remainder of ¼ cup corn kernels and sugar, stirring with heatproof rubber spatula to combine. Do this quickly, and then cover pan with lid. To keep popcorn from burning, shake pan while kernels pop. When popping slows to 2 to 3 seconds between pops, remove pan from heat and pour popcorn into a very large bowl. Sprinkle with salt, stirring and tossing popcorn kernels. Let cool completely.
• Add animal crackers, cereal, jelly beans, and chocolate candies, stirring to combine. Store in an airtight container. Portion into treat bags a few hours before serving, if desired.

FLUTTER BY
Butterfly

The
MENU

SCONE
Very Raspberry Butterfly Scones
Dragonfruit Rooibos

SAVORIES
Lemon-Dill Cucumber Butterflies
Ham & Cheese–Filled
Butterfly Cracker Sandwiches
Puff Pastry & Smoked Sausage
Butterflies with Honey-Mustard
Dipping Sauce
Sunny Afternoon Herbal Tisane

SWEETS
Butterfly Rose & Lemon
Shortbread
Stenciled Strawberry
Sandwich Cookies
Vanilla Cake Bonbons
*Beatrix Potter's Organic Herbal
Tisane Blend*

Tea Pairings by Simpson & Vail
800-282-8327 • svtea.com

*A pastel color palette and
whimsical fare provide
a charming scene for a
magical garden tea party for
butterflies to flutter about
from flower to table.*

Very Raspberry Butterfly Scones

Makes approximately 6 scones

Finely ground freeze-dried raspberries add more than just flavor to these pretty scones—they give them marvelous color, too. Pipe a trio of mascarpone cheese or clotted cream stars down the center of each scone, and serve with more of the same spread and raspberry jam on the side.

1¾ cups all-purpose flour
¼ cup granulated sugar
¼ cup finely ground freeze-dried raspberries*
½ teaspoon fine sea salt
¼ cup cold unsalted butter, cubed
1 cup plus 1 tablespoon cold heavy whipping cream
1 teaspoon vanilla extract
2 tablespoons sparkling sugar
2 tablespoons mascarpone cheese or clotted cream, softened

• Preheat oven to 400°. Line a rimmed baking sheet with parchment paper.
• In a large bowl, whisk together flour, sugar, ground raspberries, and salt. Using a pastry blender or 2 forks, cut in butter into flour mixture until it resembles coarse crumbs.
• In a small bowl, stir together 1 cup cream and vanilla extract. Gradually add to flour mixture, stirring well with a fork, just until ingredients are combined and a shaggy dough begins to form. Working gently, bring mixture together with hands until a dough forms.
• Turn out dough onto a lightly floured, surface and knead gently until smooth by patting dough and folding it in half 4 to 5 times. Using a rolling pin, roll out dough to a ¾-inch thickness. Using a 3-inch butterfly-shaped cutter dipped in flour, cut as many scones from dough as possible, rerolling scraps once. Place scones 2 inches apart on prepared baking sheet.
• Brush tops of scones with remaining 1 tablespoon cream, and sprinkle with sparkling sugar.
• Bake until scones are golden brown and a wooden pick inserted in centers comes out clean, 15 to 20 minutes. Let cool completely.
• Place mascarpone cheese or clotted cream in a piping bag fitted with a small star tip (Wilton #21). Holding the piping bag perpendicular to scone, pipe 3 stars of mascarpone cheese or clotted cream down center of each scone. Serve immediately.

We used a small food processor.

RECOMMENDED CONDIMENTS:
Clotted cream
Raspberry jam

Lemon-Dill Cucumber Butterflies

Makes 12

Children don't have to know just how nutritious these charming, tasty butterflies actually are.

12 (1-inch) celery pieces*
¼ cup cream cheese, softened
½ teaspoon finely chopped fresh dill
¼ teaspoon fresh lemon zest
⅜ teaspoon fine sea salt, divided
⅛ teaspoon ground black pepper
12 thin slices cucumber**, halved
24 thin slices green onion (approximately 1x¹⁄₁₆ inch)
12 (1-inch) strips pimiento

• Referring to how-to photographs on page 129, cut a lengthwise portion from the bottom (rounded side) of each celery piece to make them sit flat.
• In a small bowl, stir together cream cheese, dill, lemon zest, ⅛ teaspoon salt, and pepper. Transfer mixture to a small piping bag; cut a ¼-inch-wide hole in tip. Pipe approximately 1 teaspoon cream cheese mixture into each celery piece.
• On each celery piece, place 2 green onion pieces at one end of cream cheese mixture to create antennae, letting approximately ¾ inch of onion pieces extend over the edge. Press 2 cucumber slice halves, rounded edges together, into cream cheese mixture. Cover cream cheese mixture with a pimiento strip. Serve immediately, or loosely cover and refrigerate for up to 30 minutes. Just before serving, lightly sprinkle with remaining ¼ teaspoon salt.

*Using celery stalks with a slightly wide groove will make celery pieces easier to fill.
**For even slices, we used the #2 setting on a mandoline.

"Happiness is like a butterfly, the more you chase it, the more it will evade you, but if you notice the other things around you, it will gently come and sit on your shoulder." —HENRY DAVID THOREAU

Ham & Cheese–Filled Butterfly Cracker Sandwiches

Makes 16

Purchased butterfly-shaped crackers, seasoned and baked for a few minutes, replace the usual bread in these delightful tea sandwiches that are filled with a cheesy ham salad.

32 butterfly-shaped crackers*
1 tablespoon vegetable oil or avocado oil
1¾ teaspoon ranch seasoning*, divided
1 teaspoon dried parsley
¾ cup finely chopped hickory smoked maple ham
½ cup finely shredded sharp Cheddar cheese (2 ounces)
5 tablespoons mayonnaise
1 tablespoon finely chopped celery

• Preheat oven to 375°.
• Place crackers on a large, rimmed baking sheet. Lightly brush tops of crackers with oil and sprinkle with 1 teaspoon ranch seasoning and parsley.
• Bake just until lightly browned, approximately 4 minutes. Let cool completely.
• In a medium bowl, combine ham, cheese, mayonnaise, celery, and remaining ¾ teaspoon ranch seasoning; stir well.
• Turn 16 crackers over (seasoned sides down). Spoon approximately 1 tablespoon ham mixture onto each of those crackers, spreading to conform mixture to butterfly shape. Top with remaining crackers, seasoned side up, pressing slightly. Serve immediately, or cover and refrigerate for up to 30 minutes.

We used Pepperidge Farm Golden Butter Crackers and Hidden Valley Original Ranch Seasoning Salad Dressing & Recipe Mix.

"The butterfly is a flying flower. The flower is a tethered butterfly."

—PONCE DENIS ÉCOUCHARD LEBRUN

Puff Pastry & Smoked Sausage Butterflies

Makes 18

Easy to prepare and ridiculously good, these savory winged pastries might very well become a crowd favorite, especially when served with honey-sweetened mustard.

1 (17.3-ounce) package frozen puff pastry, slightly thawed
1 large egg
2 teaspoons water
18 cocktail-size smoked link sausages*
2 teaspoons everything bagel seasoning
Honey-Mustard Dipping Sauce (recipe follows)

• Preheat oven to 400°. Line 2 large baking sheets with parchment paper.
• On a lightly floured surface, unroll pastry sheets. Roll each pastry sheet into a 10-inch square. Using a 3-inch butterfly-shaped cutter, cut 9 shapes from each pastry sheet. Place shapes 1 inch apart on prepared baking sheets.
• In a small bowl, whisk together egg and 2 teaspoons water to make an egg wash. Brush pastry butterflies with egg wash. Place a sausage in the center of each butterfly, pressing slightly into place. Sprinkle pastry wings with everything bagel seasoning.
• Bake until pastries are puffed and golden, approximately 10 minutes. Serve warm with Honey-Mustard Dipping Sauce.

We used Hillshire Farm Lit'l Smokies.

Honey-Mustard Dipping Sauce

Makes approximately ½ cup

Two simple ingredients combine for a yummy dipping sauce that works quite well with our Puff Pastry & Smoked Sausage Butterflies.

⅓ cup prepared yellow mustard
2 tablespoons honey

• In a small bowl, whisk together mustard and honey. Use immediately.

Butterfly Rose & Lemon Shortbread

Makes approximately 26

Small logs of lemon-flavored shortbread, piped with a luscious lemon buttercream topping, are easily dressed up like butterflies with the addition of lemon zest strips for antennae and candied rose petals for wings.

1¾ cups all-purpose flour
1 cup confectioner's sugar
3 teaspoons fresh lemon zest
½ teaspoon fine sea salt
½ cup unsalted butter, cold, diced into tiny cubes
2 tablespoons fresh lemon juice
Lemon Buttercream (recipe follows)
Garnish: 2 (1-inch-long) strips fresh lemon zest* and
　4 Sugared Rose Petals (recipe follows) per cookie

• Preheat oven to 350°. Line 2 rimmed baking sheets with parchment paper.
• In the work bowl of a food processor, pulse together flour, confectioners' sugar, lemon zest, and salt. Add butter and lemon juice, processing until mixture resembles sand, 30 to 60 seconds.
• Turn mixture out onto a clean surface, and using hands, press into a dough ball and flatten to a disk.
• On a well-floured surface and using a rolling pin, roll out dough to a ½-inch thickness. Using a large chef's knife or a bench knife, cut dough into 2x½-inch rectangles. Place dough rectangles, evenly spaced, on prepared baking sheets. Freeze until dough is firm to the touch, approximately 15 minutes.
• Bake frozen cookies, one pan at a time, until cookies are dry to the touch and bottoms just begin to turn golden, 18 to 23 minutes. Let cool completely. Store in an airtight container until ready to assemble and serve.
• Place Lemon Buttercream in a piping bag fitted with a medium-large round tip (Wilton #10). Pipe a line of buttercream down center of each cookie.
• To garnish each cookie as a butterfly, insert 2 lemon zest strips into buttercream for antennae and 4 Sugared Rose Petals for wings.

We used a channel knife to create long, thin strips of lemon zest.

Lemon Buttercream

Makes approximately 1½ cups

Fresh lemon zest and juice give this pipeable topping enchanting zing.

½ cup unsalted butter, softened
4 cups confectioners' sugar
½ teaspoon fine sea salt
2 teaspoons fresh lemon zest
2 tablespoons fresh lemon juice

• In a large bowl, beat together butter, confectioners' sugar, salt, lemon zest, and lemon juice with a mixer at low speed until combined, scraping down sides of bowl as necessary. Increase speed to high, and beat until light and fluffy. Use immediately.

MAKE-AHEAD TIP: Buttercream can be made up to a day in advance, covered tightly, and refrigerated. Let come to room temperature and beat at high speed with a mixer for 1 minute before using.

Sugared Rose Petals

Makes 104

Since sugaring more than 100 fresh rose petals can be a bit time consuming, why not enlist the help of children or friends and make it a fun assembly line? While one person gently removes the petals from their stems, another can paint them with egg wash, and someone else can sprinkle them with sugar.

4 large pasteurized egg whites, room temperature
4 tablespoons water
104 small organic rose petals*
4 cups superfine sugar or castor sugar

• Line a rimmed baking sheet with parchment paper.
• In a small bowl, whisk together egg whites and 4 tablespoons water to make an egg wash.
• Referring to how-to photographs on page 130 and using tweezers to hold each petal, brush egg wash over both sides of petal and sprinkle petal generously with sugar. Place petals on prepared baking sheet. Let dry overnight. Once dry, store in a single layer in an airtight container at room temperature up to 3 months.

We used yellow spray roses. Only pesticide-free roses are recommended.

Stenciled Strawberry Sandwich Cookies
Makes approximately 10

Strawberry gelatin gives these cookies their pink hue and bright flavor, while finely ground freeze-dried strawberries impart fresh berry taste to the buttercream filling without making it too wet. A perfectly positioned stencil and a dusting of confectioners' sugar create a delicate butterfly design on the tops of these sweet treats.

½ cup unsalted butter, room temperature
½ cup granulated sugar
⅓ cup strawberry gelatin
2 large eggs
1 teaspoon vanilla extract
1¾ cups all-purpose flour
½ teaspoon baking powder
¼ teaspoon fine sea salt
Strawberry Buttercream Filling (recipe follows)
Garnish: 1 small butterfly stencil* and confectioners'
    sugar

• Preheat oven to 325°. Line a rimmed baking sheet with parchment paper.
• In a large bowl, beat together butter, sugar, and gelatin with a mixer at medium speed until light and fluffy. Beat in eggs and vanilla extract.
• In a medium bowl, whisk together flour, baking powder, and salt. Add to butter mixture, beating just until combined. Using a 1-tablespoon levered scoop, divide dough into 20 equal portions. Using floured hands, roll each portion into a ball, and place at least 2 inches apart on prepared baking sheet.
• Bake until cookies are set, 8 to 10 minutes. Let rest on baking sheet for 5 minutes before transferring cookies to a wire rack to let cool completely.
• Place Strawberry Buttercream Filling in a piping bag fitted with a large star tip (Wilton #1M). Pipe a buttercream rosette onto flat side of 10 cookies. Cover each with a remaining cookie, flat side down, to make 10 sandwich cookies.

• Just before serving, garnish each cookie by placing
a small butterfly stencil over cookie and dusting gently
with confectioners' sugar, if desired. Carefully lift stencil
to remove it from cookie. Discard excess confectioners' sugar from stencil before using stencil on another
cookie. Serve immediately.

*We used 3½-inch round butterfly cake stencils from Designer Stencils®,
available from amazon.com.

MAKE-AHEAD TIP: Sandwich cookies can be assembled early
in the day, placed in a single layer in an airtight container, and
refrigerated. Let come to room temperature before garnishing
and serving.

Strawberry Buttercream Filling
Makes approximately 1½ cups

This traditional buttercream gets amazing fruity notes
from freeze-dried strawberries. So the filling is easy to pipe,
be sure to grind the berries very finely.

1 cup unsalted butter, softened
½ teaspoon vanilla extract
2 cups confectioners' sugar
5 tablespoons finely ground freeze-dried strawberries*

• In a large mixing bowl, beat together butter and
vanilla extract with a mixer at medium speed until
creamy and smooth.
• In a medium bowl, whisk together confectioners'
sugar and ground strawberries. Add to butter, beating
at low speed until combined, scraping down sides of
bowl as necessary. Increase speed to high, and beat
until light and fluffy. Use immediately.

*We used a small food processor.

MAKE-AHEAD TIP: Buttercream can be made up to a day in
advance, covered tightly, and refrigerated. Let come to room
temperature and beat at high speed with a mixer for 1 minute
before using.

Vanilla Cake Bonbons

Makes 40

Edible wafer paper butterflies perch atop cake bonbons coated with vanilla-flavored melting wafers. Children will enjoy helping crumble the cake used for the centers of these sweet treats.

1¼ cups cake flour
1 teaspoon baking powder
¼ teaspoon fine sea salt
⅔ cup unsalted butter, softened, divided
⅔ cup granulated sugar
1 large egg, room temperature
5 teaspoons vanilla extract, divided
½ cup plus 2 tablespoons whole milk, room
    temperature, divided
2 cups confectioners' sugar
1 cup teal blue sanding sugar
25 ounces white vanilla-flavored melting wafers*
Edible wafer paper butterfly-shaped cake decorations**

• Preheat oven to 350°. Spray an 8-inch round cake pan with baking spray with flour. Line 2 rimmed baking sheets with parchment paper.
• In a small bowl, sift together flour, baking powder, and salt.
• In a large bowl, beat ⅓ cup butter until creamy. Beat in granulated sugar until fluffy, 1 to 2 minutes. Beat in egg and 1 tablespoon vanilla extract. Add flour mixture to butter mixture, alternating with ½ cup milk, beginning and ending with flour mixture, beating until well combined. Spoon batter into prepared pan.

• Bake until a wooden pick comes out clean, 20 to 22 minutes. Let cake cool completely in pan on a wire rack. Crumble cake when cooled, making sure there are no large lumps.
• Meanwhile, in another large bowl, beat remaining ⅓ cup butter at medium speed with a mixer until creamy, approximately 2 minutes. Beat in confectioners' sugar, remaining 2 tablespoons milk, and remaining 2 teaspoons vanilla extract, beginning at low speed and increasing to high speed, for 3 minutes. Beat in crumbled cake at low speed until combined.
• Using a 1-tablespoon levered scoop, portion cake mixture and roll each portion into a ball. Place balls on a prepared baking sheet. Refrigerate for 2 hours or freeze for 1 hour.
• Using hands, re-roll chilled cake balls to smooth and compact. Return cake balls to baking sheet and refrigerate until ready to coat, at least 30 minutes.
• Place sanding sugar in a small bowl.
• Place melting wafers in a 4-cup microwave-safe, liquid-measuring cup. Heat in the microwave on high in 30 second intervals until wafers melt and are smooth, stirring between intervals.
• Remove only 2 or 3 cake balls from the refrigerator at a time. Dip one cake ball at a time into melted coating, turning gently with a fork, until cake ball is completely covered. Gently pierce cake ball with fork, remove coated cake ball, gently shaking off excess melted coating. Using a knife, gently push cake ball off fork and onto remaining prepared baking sheet. Let stand just until coating begins to lose its shine.
• Meanwhile, transfer remaining melted coating to a piping bag fitted with a small round tip (Wilton #1). Cover tip and set aside.
• Insert a wooden pick into each cake ball. Place cake ball into sanding sugar and gently press into sugar (do not roll the cake ball around in the sugar). Remove from sugar and return to prepared baking sheet. Let stand until coating is set. Gently twist set cake pops to remove wooden picks.
• Pipe a dot of melted coating onto each coated cake ball to cover hole. Place a butterfly decoration on coating dot, pressing gently to adhere. Serve immediately, or store in a single layer in an airtight container and refrigerate until needed, up to 2 days. Serve cold or at room temperature.

We used Ghirardelli.
**Edible wafer paper butterfly cake decorations are available from amazon.com.*

FIT FOR
Royal-tea

The
MENU

SCONE
Raspberry-Crowned
White Chocolate Mini Scones
Winter Palace Marzipan Rooibos

SAVORIES
Fruit Salad Jewelry Boxes
Apple Chicken Salad Puffs
Hazelnut-Chocolate PB&J Crowns
Decaf Peach Apricot Black Tea

SWEETS
Sparkling Lemon Mini Cupcakes
Pink Almond Crinkle Cookies
Jeweled Meringue Kisses
Bella Coola Fruit & Herbal Tea

Tea Pairings by The Tea Shoppe
304-413-0890 • theteashoppewv.com

*Gather favorite friends to don
frilly dresses, shiny tiaras, and
elegant jewels for an afternoon
tea that every princess-in-
training is sure to love.*

Raspberry-Crowned White Chocolate Mini Scones

Makes 20

A fresh raspberry is the crown jewel of these sweet scones that are studded with white chocolate and topped with a pretty dollop of slightly sweet whipped cream, thus eliminating the need for any other condiments.

2½ cups all-purpose flour*
¼ cup plus 1½ teaspoons granulated sugar, divided
1 tablespoon baking powder
2 teaspoons cornstarch
½ teaspoon fine sea salt
½ cup frozen unsalted butter, coarsely grated
2 ounces white baking chocolate, finely chopped
¾ cup cold heavy cream, divided
½ teaspoon vanilla extract
Sweetened Whipped Cream (recipe follows)
20 fresh raspberries

• Preheat oven to 375°. Line a rimmed baking sheet with parchment paper.
• In a large bowl, whisk together flour, ¼ cup sugar, baking powder, cornstarch, and salt. Stir in grated butter and white chocolate.
• In a small bowl, stir together ½ cup plus 2 tablespoons heavy cream and vanilla extract. Add to flour mixture, stirring just until ingredients are combined and a shaggy dough begins to form. Working gently, bring mixture together with hands until a dough forms. (Dough will be firm once it comes together. If dough won't come together, add more cream, 1 tablespoon at a time, until it does.)
• Turn dough out onto a lightly floured surface, and knead gently until smooth by patting dough and folding it in half 3 to 4 times. Using a rolling pin, roll out dough to a ½-inch thickness. Using a 1¾-inch round cutter dipped in flour, cut 20 scones from dough, rerolling scraps as needed. Place scones 2 inches apart on prepared baking sheet.
• Brush tops of scones with remaining 2 tablespoons heavy cream, and sprinkle with remaining 1½ teaspoons sugar.
• Bake until edges of scones are golden brown and a wooden pick inserted in centers comes out clean, 18 to 20 minutes. Let scones cool completely.

• Just before serving, place Sweetened Whipped Cream in a piping bag fitted with a large star tip (Wilton #1M), and pipe an upright rosette on top of each scone. Top each cream rosette with a fresh raspberry, if desired. Serve immediately.

Spoon flour into measuring cup without packing and then scrape off excess with a straight edge to level.

Sweetened Whipped Cream

Makes 2 cups

Perfect for piping on top of scones, this tasty topping will have teatime guests oohing and aahing.

1 cup cold heavy whipping cream
2 tablespoons confectioners' sugar
¼ teaspoon vanilla extract

• In a deep bowl, beat together cream, confectioners' sugar, and vanilla extract at high speed with a mixer until thickened and creamy. Use immediately.

Fruit Salad Jewelry Boxes

Makes 8

Fresh watermelon squares serve as vessels for yogurt with a colorful topping of fruit salad.

½ seedless watermelon, chilled
1¼ cups vanilla Greek yogurt
¼ teaspoon fresh orange zest
⅓ cup finely chopped strawberries
⅓ cup finely chopped green grapes
¼ cup finely chopped kiwi
8 blueberries

• Cut away watermelon rind and discard. Using a sharp knife and a ruler, cut 8 (1-inch) thick slices from watermelon. Cut a 2-inch square from each slice. Using a melon baller, scoop out center of each watermelon square to make a "box." Blot dry with paper towels.

• In a small bowl, stir together yogurt and orange zest. Fill wells of watermelon boxes with yogurt mixture.
• In another small bowl, stir together strawberries, grapes, and kiwi. Top yogurt mixture with fruit mixture. Top each with a blueberry. Store in a covered container in the refrigerator and serve within an hour.

MAKE-AHEAD TIP: Watermelon boxes can be made one day in advance and stored in a covered container in the refrigerator.

Apple Chicken Salad Puffs

Makes 20

Choux pastry puffs are an elegant presentation for chicken salad.

¾ cup water
6 tablespoons unsalted butter, cubed
2 teaspoons granulated sugar
¼ teaspoon fine sea salt
1 cup all-purpose flour
4 large eggs, room temperature, divided
3 tablespoons mayonnaise
2 cups spring mix lettuce
Apple Chicken Salad (recipe follows)
Garnish: sea salt flakes

• Preheat oven to 400°. Line 2 rimmed baking sheets with parchment paper.
• In a medium saucepan, combine water, butter, sugar, and salt. Cook over medium heat until butter melts. Add flour all at once, stirring vigorously with a wooden spoon. Cook and stir until dough pulls away from sides of pan, 1 to 2 minutes. Remove pan from heat, and let stand for 2 minutes, stirring a few times to cool dough.
• Transfer dough to a large bowl. Add 3 eggs, one at the time, beating with a mixer at medium speed until well incorporated. (Dough should be shiny and smooth.) Transfer dough to a piping bag fitted with a large round tip (Sunny Side Up Bakery #2A or Ateco #806). Pipe dough in a coiled or circular pattern in 1½-inch mounds, 2 inches apart, onto prepared baking sheets. Pat dough peaks down with a damp finger.
• In a small bowl, whisk remaining egg until combined. Brush dough lightly with egg. Garnish tops with a sprinkle of salt flakes, if desired.
• Bake until golden brown, 20 to 25 minutes. (To check for doneness, pull apart a puff. Insides should be dry.) Transfer puffs to a wire rack. Using a skewer or the tip of

a pointed knife, poke a small hole in sides of each puff to allow steam to escape. Let cool completely.

• Using a serrated knife, cut each puff in half horizontally. Spread a thin layer of mayonnaise onto each cut bottom half of puff. Arrange a few lettuce leaves on top of mayonnaise. Place a scoop of chicken salad on top of lettuce. Cover with top half of puffs. Serve immediately or store in a covered container in the refrigerator for up to 2 hours.

MAKE-AHEAD TIP: Cooled puffs can be placed in an airtight container and frozen for up to a month. Thaw before using.

Apple Chicken Salad
Makes 3 cups

Chopped red apple—choose your favorite variety!—looks like little jewels in this teatime staple and gives it delightful bursts of sweetness. While the lemon juice in the chicken salad should keep the fresh fruit from turning brown too quickly when refrigerated, we recommend serving it within a day for optimal color and texture.

2½ cups coarsely chopped roast chicken
¾ cup small diced red apple
½ cup plus 1 tablespoon mayonnaise
2 teaspoons fresh lemon juice
¼ teaspoon fine sea salt
⅛ teaspoon ground black pepper

• In the work bowl of a food processor, pulse chicken until finely chopped. (Don't over process, or chicken meat will be gummy.)
• In a large bowl, stir together finely chopped chicken, apple, mayonnaise, lemon juice, salt, and pepper. Use immediately, or transfer to a covered container, refrigerate, and use within a day.

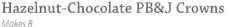

"You may be a princess or the richest woman in the world, but you cannot be more than a lady."

—LADY RANDOLPH CHURCHILL

Hazelnut-Chocolate PB&J Crowns

Makes 8

Traditional peanut butter and jelly sandwiches get the royal treatment with the addition of chocolate-hazelnut spread, elegant sprinkles, and the requisite crown shape.

8 slices firm white sandwich bread, frozen
8 slices multi-grain white bread, frozen
½ cup chocolate-hazelnut spread
½ cup unsalted butter, softened
½ cup creamy peanut butter
½ cup seedless strawberry jam
Garnish: candy stars* and sprinkle mix*

• Using a 3-inch crown-shaped cutter*, cut 16 shapes from frozen bread, discarding scraps. To prevent bread from drying out, cover with damp paper towels or place in a resealable plastic bag, and let thaw at room temperature.

• Place chocolate-hazelnut spread in a piping bag fitted with a small round tip (Wilton #5)**. Place butter in a piping bag fitted with a smaller round tip (Wilton #4)**.
• Using an offset spatula, spread an even layer of peanut butter onto multi-grain bread shapes, leaving a ½-inch border. Spread an even layer of strawberry jam over peanut butter layer. Pipe chocolate-hazelnut spread onto ½-inch border along edges of crown shapes, encasing peanut butter and jam. Cover each with a white bread crown. Pipe butter around edges of white bread crowns to outline shape and a row of dots along bottoms of crowns. Garnish butter outline of each sandwich with a candy star and sprinkle mix, if desired. Keep in a covered container at room temperature and serve within 2 hours.

We used candy stars from Sunny Side Up Bakery® Princess Sprinkle Blend, Sunny Side Up Bakery® Edible Glitter & Sugar Blend, and a crown cutter from a Sunny Side Up Bakery set, available from Hobby Lobby, hobbylobby.com.
**Alternatively, cut a small hole in the end of piping bag.*

Sparkling Lemon Mini Cupcakes

Makes 39

Bursting with vibrant lemon flavor, these lovely cupcakes are sure to garner accolades, especially when piped with a pretty rosette of complementary frosting, garnished with sparkling sugar, and set in a holder made from the edging of a paper doily.

½ cup unsalted butter, softened
1 cup granulated sugar
1 tablespoon fresh lemon zest
2 large eggs
½ teaspoon lemon extract
⅛ teaspoon vanilla extract
1½ cups cake flour
1½ teaspoons baking powder
¼ teaspoon fine sea salt
½ cup whole milk
Very Lemon Buttercream (recipe follows)
Garnish: white sparkling sugar

- Preheat oven to 350°. Line 2 (24-well) mini muffin pans with 39 mini baking cups.
- In a large bowl, beat together butter, sugar, and lemon zest at high speed with a mixer until light and fluffy, approximately 3 minutes, scraping down sides of bowl as needed. Beat in eggs, one at a time, until incorporated. Beat in extracts.
- In a medium bowl, whisk together flour, baking powder, and salt. Add flour mixture and milk to butter mixture, alternately in thirds, beginning and ending with flour mixture, scraping down sides of bowl as necessary. (Don't overbeat, or cupcakes will be dry.)
- Using a 2-teaspoon levered scoop, divide cake batter among prepared wells of muffin pans. Tap pans on countertop a few times to settle batter and reduce air bubbles. (Don't fill bake cups with more than 2 teaspoons batter, or batter will spill over during baking.)
- Bake until cupcake edges are very light golden brown and a wooden pick inserted in centers comes out clean, 8 to 12 minutes. (Don't overbake, or cupcakes will be dry.) Transfer cupcakes to a wire cooling rack. Let cool completely.
- Place Very Lemon Buttercream in a piping bag fitted with a large open star tip (Wilton #1M). Pipe a swirl of buttercream onto each cupcake.
- Garnish with white sparkling sugar just before serving, if desired.

MAKE-AHEAD TIP: Cupcakes can be baked a day in advance, frosted, and stored in an airtight container in the refrigerator. For best flavor, let come to room temperature before serving.

Very Lemon Buttercream

Makes 3½ cups

Fresh lemon juice gives this frosting its marvelous punch of citrus flavor.

4½ cups confectioners' sugar
1 cup unsalted butter, softened
3 tablespoons fresh lemon juice
¼ teaspoon fine sea salt

- In a large bowl, beat together confectioners' sugar, butter, lemon juice, and salt beginning at low speed with a mixer and then increasing to high speed until light and fluffy. Use immediately.

Pink Almond Crinkle Cookies

Makes approximately 34

Dainty and oh-so tempting, these cookies get color and taste from pomegranate juice and a pair of extracts. Resist the urge to bake them longer than the recipe indicates, as they will firm up when cooled.

¼ cup unsalted butter, softened
¼ cup canola oil
¾ cup granulated sugar
1 large egg, room temperature
½ teaspoon almond extract
¼ teaspoon vanilla extract
2 tablespoons pomegranate juice
Pink gel food coloring
1½ cups all-purpose flour
¼ teaspoon baking powder
¼ teaspoon baking soda
¼ teaspoon fine sea salt
1½ cups confectioners' sugar

• In a large bowl, beat together butter and oil at high speed with a mixer until light and creamy, approximately 3 minutes. Beat in egg until incorporated. Beat in extracts and pomegranate juice just until incorporated. Beat in desired amount of food coloring.
• In a medium bowl, whisk together flour, baking powder, baking soda, and salt. Add to butter mixture all at once, beating until combined. Cover bowl with plastic wrap and refrigerate for 1 hour. (This will make dough easier to handle.)
• Preheat oven to 350°. Line 2 rimmed baking sheets with parchment paper.
• Place confectioners' sugar in a wide, shallow bowl.
• Using a 2-teaspoon levered scoop, drop balls of dough into confectioners' sugar. Roll dough balls in confectioners' sugar to coat generously and completely. Place 2 inches apart on prepared baking sheets.
• Bake cookies until crackled and very lightly browned on bottoms for 8 to 10 minutes. (Cookies will be moist and might seem underdone but will firm and crisp when cooled.) Let cookies sit for 1 minute on baking sheets before removing to wire racks to cool completely. Store in an airtight container at room temperature with layers separated by wax paper for up to 2 days.

Jeweled Meringue Kisses

Makes 50

Light and airy drops of vanilla-flavored meringue are dressed to the nines with edible glitter and pearlized sprinkles. The meringues' crispy texture is achieved by letting them dry for 6 to 8 hours in the oven.

4 large egg whites, room temperature
½ teaspoon cream of tartar
⅔ cup granulated sugar
6 tablespoons confectioners' sugar
¼ teaspoon fine sea salt
1½ teaspoons vanilla extract
Garnish: edible pink glitter hearts* and
    pearlized sprinkles*

• Preheat oven to 250°. Line 2 rimmed baking sheets with parchment paper.
• In a large mixing bowl, beat together egg whites and cream of tartar at high speed with a mixer until soft peaks begin to form. Beat in sugars and salt. Continue to beat at high speed until stiff peaks form and meringue is shiny, approximately 3 minutes. Fold in vanilla extract.
• Transfer mixture to a piping bag fitted with a very large open star tip (Sunny Side Up Bakery #8B). Pipe 50 drops, evenly spaced, onto prepared baking sheets. Garnish with glitter hearts and sprinkles, if desired.
• Bake for 50 to 60 minutes, being careful not to let meringues brown. Turn oven off and keep door open until hot air escapes. Close oven door, and let meringues sit overnight in oven with door closed to dry out and form a lightly airy texture. The next day, store at room temperature in an airtight container with layers separated by wax paper.

We used Wilton.

KITCHEN TIP: *To keep parchment paper in place while piping meringues, pipe small dots of meringue mixture on baking sheets at corners before placing parchment sheet.*

TIME FOR A
Fiesta

The
MENU

SCONE
Mexican Hot Chocolate Scones

Passion Flamenco

SAVORIES
Taco Salad Canapés

Street Corn

Chicken Taquitos with
Avocado Crema

*Lemon Mango Punch Fruit
& Herbal Tea*

SWEETS
Tres Leches Cupcakes

Mini Churros with
Milk Chocolate Sauce

Piñata Sugar Cookies

Piña Colada Fruit & Herbal Tea

Tea Pairings by The Tea Shoppe
304-413-0890 • theteashoppewv.com

*Children will fall in love
with the vibrant decorations
and Latin American–inspired
cuisine at this joyous
afternoon-tea celebration.*

Mexican Hot Chocolate Scones

Makes approximately 12

Best served slightly warm with lashings of clotted cream and guava jelly, these delightful, chocolaty treats, sporting a nice dose of cinnamon, evoke the flavors of the traditional hot beverage.

2⅔ cups all-purpose flour
⅓ cup unsweetened cocoa powder
¼ cup granulated sugar
4 teaspoons baking powder
1 teaspoon ground cinnamon
½ teaspoon fine sea salt
½ cup cold unsalted butter, cubed
½ cup miniature semisweet chocolate chips
1 cup cold heavy whipping cream
1 large egg, lightly beaten
2 teaspoons turbinado sugar

• Preheat oven to 375°. Line a rimmed baking sheet with parchment paper.
• In a large bowl, whisk together flour, cocoa powder, granulated sugar, baking powder, cinnamon, and salt. Using a pastry blender or 2 forks, cut butter into flour mixture until it resembles coarse crumbs. Stir in chocolate chips. Using a fork, stir in cream just until a shaggy dough starts to come together. Working gently, bring mixture together with hands until a dough forms in the bowl.
• Turn dough out onto a lightly floured surface, and knead gently until smooth by patting dough and folding it in half 3 to 4 times. Using a rolling pin, roll dough to a ¾-inch thickness. Using a 2¼-inch fluted round cutter dipped in flour, cut as many scones as possible from dough without twisting cutter, rerolling once. Place scones 2 inches apart on prepared baking sheet. Freeze for 10 minutes. Brush tops of scones with egg and sprinkle with turbinado sugar.
• Bake until scones are golden brown, 16 to 20 minutes. Let cool on baking sheet for 5 minutes. Serve warm.

RECOMMENDED CONDIMENTS:
Clotted cream
Guava jelly

Taco Salad Canapés

Makes 24

Ground beef, cooked with Mexican spices and mixed with refried beans, fills charming edible cups made from wonton wrappers. Top with lettuce, cheese, sour cream, and store-bought pico de gallo for a tea-size ode to traditional taco salad. If pico de gallo isn't available or palatable, substitute finely chopped tomato.

24 wonton wrappers
5 ounces lean ground beef
2 tablespoons minced red bell pepper
2 tablespoons minced white onion
1 tablespoon tomato paste
¼ teaspoon fine sea salt
⅛ teaspoon ground cumin
⅛ teaspoon ground coriander
⅛ teaspoon smoked paprika
⅛ teaspoon chili powder
⅛ teaspoon ground black pepper
2 tablespoons canned refried beans
¼ cup shredded iceberg lettuce
¼ cup grated Mexican cheese blend
¼ cup sour cream
¼ cup prepared pico de gallo

• Preheat oven to 350°. Lightly spray a 24-well mini muffin pan with cooking spray.
• Using a 2⅞-inch round cutter, cut a circle from each wonton wrapper. Press wonton circles into wells of prepared muffin pan. Lightly spray wonton circles with cooking spray. Bake until golden brown and crisp, 6 to 7 minutes. Let cool in pan for 5 minutes before removing to a wire rack to let cool completely.
• In a medium skillet, cook beef over medium-high heat, stirring occasionally, until browned, approximately 5 minutes. Drain fat from beef, if desired, and return to skillet. Stir in bell pepper, onion, tomato paste, salt, cumin, coriander, paprika, chili powder, and black pepper. Cook mixture until peppers and onions are soft, approximately 5 minutes more. Stir in refried beans.

• Divide beef mixture among prepared wonton cups. Top with lettuce, cheese, sour cream, and pico de gallo. Serve immediately.

MAKE-AHEAD TIPS: Wonton cups can be prepared early in the day and stored in an airtight container. Fill just before serving. Beef mixture can be prepared a day in advance, cooled, placed in an airtight container, and refrigerated. Let mixture come to room temperature or warm mixture slightly before using, if desired.

Street Corn

Makes 16

While corn on the cob is almost never served for afternoon tea, this iteration is perfectly portioned for the occasion and bursting with traditional Mexican flavors, such as a lightly spiced lime mayonnaise, crumbled cotija cheese, and fresh cilantro. Frilled wooden picks make serving and eating easier and add color to the plate.

4 ears fresh corn, shucked
¼ cup mayonnaise
¼ teaspoon fresh lime zest
1½ teaspoons fresh lime juice
¼ teaspoon chili powder
¼ cup crumbled cotija cheese
2 tablespoons chopped fresh cilantro
Garnish: chili powder

• Heat a grill or grill pan to medium-high heat. Grill corn until browned on all sides and tender, 8 to 10 minutes. Cut corn crosswise into 1½-inch pieces.
• In a small bowl, combine mayonnaise, lime zest, lime juice, and chili powder. Brush corn with mayonnaise mixture. Roll corn in cheese. Sprinkle corn with chopped cilantro.
• Garnish with chili powder and insert a wooden pick into the center of each corn piece, if desired. Serve within an hour.

- In a medium bowl, combine chicken, cream cheese, and queso fresco. Working with 1 warm tortilla at a time, spoon approximately 1 scant tablespoon chicken mixture onto center of tortilla. Roll up tortilla tightly to encase filling. Using a wooden pick, secure seam. Repeat with remaining tortillas and chicken mixture.
- In a Dutch oven, heat 2 inches oil over medium heat to 350°. Add prepared tortillas to oil in batches and fry until golden brown, approximately 2 minutes. Drain on paper towels. Carefully remove toothpicks. Sprinkle with salt while still warm. Serve immediately with Avocado Crema.

To warm tortillas, wrap 4 tortillas in several dampened paper towels. Heat wrapped tortillas in a microwave oven on high just until warm, 15 to 20 seconds.

MAKE-AHEAD TIPS: *Tortillas can be assembled early in the day, stored in an airtight container, and refrigerated until ready to fry. Blot excess moisture with paper towels before frying.*

Avocado Crema
Makes 1¼ cups

Sour cream, lime zest and juice, and fresh cilantro give avocado marvelous tang in this condiment for our Chicken Taquitos, which would work equally well as a dip for tortilla chips or as a sandwich spread.

3 medium ripe avocados, halved, pitted, and peeled
¼ cup sour cream
¼ teaspoon fresh lime zest
1 tablespoon fresh lime juice
1 tablespoon chopped fresh cilantro
1 teaspoon fine sea salt
Garnish: chopped fresh cilantro

- In the work bowl of a food processor, process together avocados, sour cream, lime zest, lime juice, cilantro, and salt until smooth. Transfer mixture to a serving bowl. Serve immediately, or place a piece of plastic wrap directly onto the surface and refrigerate for up to 1 hour.
- Just before serving, garnish with chopped cilantro, if desired.

Chicken Taquitos with Avocado Crema
Makes 32

A crunchy tortilla exterior and a cheesy chicken interior make these fried, savory bites truly irresistible, especially when served with Avocado Crema.

1½ cups shredded rotisserie chicken
3 ounces cream cheese, softened
½ cup crumbled queso fresco
32 street taco corn tortillas, slightly warmed*
Vegetable oil, for frying
1 tablespoon fine sea salt
Avocado Crema (recipe follows)

Tres Leches Cupcakes

Makes 24

Tres Leches Cake, or Three Milks Cake, is an iconic Mexican dessert. While still warm, the vanilla cake is poked with a wooden skewer and brushed with a mixture of three types of dairy—usually heavy cream, sweetened condensed milk, and evaporated milk—before being topped with sweetened whipped cream once cooled. These diminutive versions of this traditional treat are perfect for afternoon tea.

½ cup unsalted butter, softened
1 cup granulated sugar
2 large eggs, room temperature
½ teaspoon vanilla extract
1½ cups all-purpose flour
½ teaspoon baking powder
¼ teaspoon baking soda
¼ teaspoon kosher salt
¼ teaspoon ground cinnamon
¾ cup whole buttermilk
⅓ cup sweetened condensed milk
¼ cup heavy whipping cream
2½ tablespoons evaporated milk
Whipped Cream Frosting (recipe follows)
Garnish: thinly sliced fresh strawberries

• Preheat oven to 350°. Line a 24-well mini muffin pan with baking cups.
• In a large bowl, beat together butter and sugar at medium speed with a mixer until fluffy, stopping occasionally to scrape down sides of bowl. Add eggs, one at a time, beating well after each addition. Beat in vanilla extract.
• In a medium bowl, combine flour, baking powder, baking soda, and salt. Add flour mixture to butter mixture, alternating with buttermilk, beginning and ending with flour mixture, beating until well combined.
• Using a heaping 2-tablespoon levered scoop, divide batter among wells of prepared pan. (There may be batter left over.) Tap pan on countertop several times to level batter.
• Bake until tops are dry, and a wooden pick inserted in centers comes out clean, 10 to 15 minutes. Let cupcakes cool slightly in pan, 3 to 5 minutes.
• In a medium bowl, whisk together condensed milk, cream, and evaporated milk. Using a wooden pick or skewer, poke holes in warm cupcakes. Using a pastry brush, brush slightly cooled cupcakes with milk mixture 4 times, letting milk mixture absorb into cupcakes before brushing again. Let cupcakes cool completely in pan on a wire rack. Cover, and refrigerate until ready to serve, up to a day.
• Place Whipped Cream Frosting in a piping bag fitted with a large open-star tip (Ateco #824). Pipe a rosette of frosting onto each cupcake. Serve immediately, or place in a covered container and refrigerate for up to an hour.
• Just before serving, garnish with thinly sliced strawberries, if desired.

Whipped Cream Frosting

Makes approximately 2 cups

Ideal as a frosting for Tres Leches Cupcakes, this sweet topping can also be used as a spread for scones.

1 cup heavy whipping cream, divided
¼ cup confectioners' sugar
¼ teaspoon vanilla extract

• In a medium bowl, beat cream at medium-high speed with a mixer until soft peaks form. Add confectioners' sugar and vanilla extract, beating until stiff peaks form. Use immediately.

Mini Churros

Makes 48 to 50

Log-shaped churros are the Hispanic equivalent of funnel cake, and they are often rolled in granulated sugar, cinnamon sugar, or confectioners' sugar. These fried delights are best enjoyed warm and dipped in a chocolate sauce.

¾ cup water
6 tablespoons cold unsalted butter, cubed
1 cup plus 2 tablespoons sugar, divided
½ teaspoon kosher salt
¾ cup plus 2 tablespoons all-purpose flour
2 large eggs, room temperature
Vegetable oil, for frying
Milk Chocolate Sauce (recipe follows)

• In a large saucepan, bring ¾ cup water, butter, 2 tablespoons sugar, and salt to a boil over medium-high heat, stirring occasionally. Using a wooden spoon, stir in flour. (Mixture will foam.) Cook over medium-low heat, stirring constantly, until mixture forms a thick dough and leaves a film on bottom of pan, 1 to 2 minutes. Transfer dough to a large bowl; let cool for 3 minutes. Add eggs, one at a time, beating well after each addition with a mixer at medium speed.
• Fill a large Dutch oven halfway with oil, and heat over medium-high heat until a deep-fry thermometer registers 360°.
• Place dough in a piping bag fitted with a large star tip (Wilton #1M). Holding bag 2 to 3 inches above oil, pipe 10 (2-inch) strips of dough at a time into oil, cutting dough with kitchen scissors or carefully swiping tip with an index finger to trim dough. Fry, turning occasionally, until golden brown, approximately 3 minutes, adjusting heat as needed to maintain 360°. Remove using a slotted spoon and let drain on paper towels.
• Roll warm churros in remaining 1 cup sugar*. Serve warm with Milk Chocolate Sauce.

*If desired, stir in ½ teaspoon ground cinnamon before rolling warm churros in sugar.

Milk Chocolate Sauce

Makes approximately 2 cups

Good enough to eat with a spoon, this almost pudding–like sauce is the perfect plunge for our Mini Churros.

¼ cup granulated sugar
1½ tablespoons cornstarch
1 cup whole milk
½ cup heavy whipping cream
⅔ cup milk chocolate chips
½ teaspoon vanilla extract

• In a medium saucepan, combine sugar and cornstarch. Whisk in milk and cream. Bring to a simmer over medium-high heat, stirring constantly. Reduce heat to medium-low; cook for 1 minute, stirring constantly. Remove from heat. Stir in chocolate chips and vanilla extract until chocolate melts. Serve warm.

Piñata Sugar Cookies

Makes 22 to 24

It wouldn't be a fiesta without a piñata, and these colorful cookies, which pay homage to the beloved game, are sure to please kids of all ages. For the royal icing, select four colors of gel food coloring to coordinate with the party decorations, keeping in mind that the icing colors will often darken as they dry.

1 cup unsalted butter, softened
1½ cups confectioners' sugar
1 large egg, room temperature
2 teaspoons vanilla extract
3 cups all-purpose flour
2 teaspoons baking powder
1 teaspoon kosher salt
Royal Icing (recipe follows)
4 colors gel food coloring*

• Preheat oven to 350°. Line several rimmed baking sheets with parchment paper.
• In a large bowl, beat together butter and confectioners' sugar with a mixer at medium speed until fluffy, 3 to 4 minutes, stopping to scrape down sides of bowl. Beat in egg and vanilla extract until combined.
• In a medium bowl, whisk together flour, baking powder, and salt. With mixer at low speed, gradually beat in flour mixture to butter mixture until a dough forms. Divide dough in half.
• Place half of dough on a heavily floured surface. Using a rolling pin, roll dough to a ¼-inch thickness. Using a 3-inch donkey piñata–shaped cookie cutter, cut as many shapes from dough as possible, and place, evenly spaced, on prepared baking sheets. Repeat with remaining dough half, rerolling scraps as necessary.
• Bake until tops are dry and edges are very lightly golden brown, 8 to 10 minutes. Let cool on baking sheets for 2 minutes before transferring to wire racks to let cool completely.
• Divide Royal Icing evenly among 4 bowls. Cover bowls with a damp towel to prevent icing from drying out. Tint each bowl of icing with gel food coloring until desired hue is achieved. (Most colors will darken as icing dries.) Cover each bowl with a damp towel again.

• Transfer each icing color to its own piping bag fitted with a small petal-shaped tip (Wilton #102)**.
• Starting at the bottom of each cookie, with narrow point of piping tip facing toward the piñata head and referring to how-to photographs on page 131, pipe tight "U" shapes to create a ruffled line across cookie. Repeat piping procedure with remaining royal icing colors, slightly overlapping onto previous royal icing color. Repeat as needed until cookies are completely covered with icing. Let cookies dry completely, 2 to 3 hours, before serving. Store in an airtight container with layers separated with wax paper for up to a week.

*We used Wilton Teal, Sunny Side Up Bakery Egg Yellow, and Wilton Leaf Green. To achieve the desired pink hue, we used Side Up Bakery Soft Pink plus Wilton Rose.
**If 4 identical tips are not available, place a coupler in each piping bag before adding icing, and wash and dry piping tip after each use, being sure to cover couplers with damp towels when not in use to prevent icing from drying out.

Royal Icing

Makes approximately 4 cups

Meringue powder mixed with confectioners' sugar, water, and vanilla extract is all it takes to create durable, yet tasty, decorations for cookies that can be tinted to the desired hues. Though the icing can be made in advance, it is imperative to store it in an airtight container to keep it from drying out before using.

7 cups confectioners' sugar
6 tablespoons meringue powder
½ cup water
1 teaspoon vanilla extract

• In a large bowl, beat together confectioners' sugar and meringue powder with a mixer at low speed until combined. Slowly beat in ½ cup water and vanilla extract, increasing speed to medium, until stiff peaks form, approximately 3 minutes. Store in an airtight container at room temperature for up to 3 days.

TEA WITH
Forest Friends

The MENU

SCONE

Maple Leaf Scones

Rooibos Pear Herbal Tea

SAVORIES

Cheesy Beef Pizza Turnovers

Chicken, Bacon, and Ranch
Tea Sandwiches

Mini Twice-Baked Potato "Mice"

*Handsome James Rooibos
Herbal Tea*

SWEETS

Pumpkin Cupcakes with
Molasses Frosting

S'mores Pudding Cups

Chocolate-Vanilla Pinwheels

*Carrot Cake Cupcake
Green Rooibos Tisane*

Tea Pairings by Simpson & Vail
800-282-8327 • svtea.com

*Tea party guests will delight
at the sight of a woodland table
set with whimsical wares,
decorations, and fare.*

Maple Leaf Scones
Makes approximately 18

Scones that get their rich flavor from maple extract call
for a maple leaf–shaped cutter, of course.

3 cups all-purpose flour
2 tablespoons granulated sugar
1 tablespoon baking powder
½ teaspoon kosher salt
½ cup cold unsalted butter, cubed
1¼ cups plus 1 tablespoon cold heavy whipping cream,
    divided
1 teaspoon maple extract
½ teaspoon vanilla extract
1 teaspoon sanding sugar

• Preheat oven to 375°. Line 2 rimmed baking sheets
with parchment paper.
• In the work bowl of a food processor, pulse together
flour, granulated sugar, baking powder, and salt just until
combined. Add butter, pulsing until it resembles coarse
crumbs. Transfer mixture to a large bowl.
• In a small bowl, stir together 1¼ cups cream and
extracts. Add to flour mixture, stirring until a dough starts
to form. Gather dough into a ball in the bowl.
• Turn out dough onto a lightly floured surface, and
knead gently until smooth 3 to 4 times. Using a rolling
pin, roll out dough to a ½-inch thickness. Using a
2½-inch maple leaf–shaped cutter dipped in flour,
cut 18 scones from dough without twisting cutter,
rerolling scraps only once. Place scones 1 inch apart on
prepared baking sheets. Using a sharp knife, cut several
shallow ⅛-inch-deep "veins" in scones. Freeze scones
for approximately 10 minutes.
• Brush tops of scones with remaining 1 tablespoon
cream. Sprinkle with sanding sugar.
• Bake until edges of scones are golden brown, approximately 17 minutes. Let cool slightly on baking sheets for
approximately 5 minutes. Serve warm.

RECOMMENDED CONDIMENTS:
Clotted cream
Apple butter

Cheesy Beef Pizza Turnovers

Makes 16

Give classic pizza pie a teatime makeover with a hand pie version that is packed with many of the iconic flavors of the Italian dish—tomato-based sauce, ground beef, and cheese.

1 tablespoon vegetable oil
½ pound ground beef
⅓ cup pizza sauce
½ teaspoon onion powder
¼ teaspoon kosher salt
½ cup finely shredded Cheddar cheese
1 (14.1-ounce) package refrigerated piecrust dough
1 egg
1 teaspoon water

• In a medium skillet, heat oil over medium-high heat. Add beef; cook until browned and crumbly. (Drain if necessary.) Add pizza sauce, onion powder, and salt, stirring until combined. Transfer mixture to a medium bowl and let cool for 30 minutes.
• Add cheese to cooled beef mixture, stirring until incorporated.
• Preheat oven to 425°. Line a large, rimmed baking sheet with parchment paper.
• On a lightly floured surface, unroll dough. Using a 3½-inch round cutter, cut 16 dough circles, rerolling scraps as necessary. Spoon approximately 1 tablespoon beef mixture onto bottom half of each dough circle. Lightly brush edge of dough with water. Fold dough over. Crimp edges of dough with a fork dipped in flour. Place turnovers 1 inch apart on prepared baking sheet.
• In a small bowl, whisk together egg and 1 teaspoon water to make an egg wash. Brush tops of turnovers with egg wash. Using a fork, pierce tops of turnovers.
• Bake until turnovers are golden brown, approximately 13 minutes. Let cool on a wire rack for approximately 10 minutes. Serve warm.

Chicken, Bacon, and Ranch Tea Sandwiches

Makes 12

This savory chicken salad, laced with chopped bacon and ranch dip, will delight even the pickiest of eaters.

5 tablespoons mayonnaise, divided
2 tablespoons sour cream
2 teaspoons ranch dip mix*
1½ cups finely chopped cooked chicken
⅓ cup finely chopped cooked bacon
6 slices butter bread*

• In a medium bowl, whisk together 3 tablespoons mayonnaise, sour cream, and dip mix until blended. Add chicken and bacon, stirring until combined.
• Spread remaining 2 tablespoons mayonnaise in a thin layer onto bread slices. Spread one-third of chicken mixture onto mayonnaise side of 1 bread slice. Top with another bread slice, mayonnaise side down. Repeat with remaining bread slices and remaining chicken mixture.
• Using a serrated knife in a gentle sawing motion, trim and discard crusts from sandwiches. Cut each sandwich into 4 finger sandwiches. Serve immediately, or cover with damp paper towels, place in a covered container, and refrigerate for up to an hour.

We used Hidden Valley Original Ranch Dips Mix and Pepperidge Farm Butter Bread.

"There is a serene and settled majesty to woodland scenery that enters into the soul and delights and elevates it, and fills it with noble inclinations."

—WASHINGTON IRVING

Mini Twice-Baked Potato "Mice"

Makes 24

Transform petite twice-baked potatoes into cute little "mice" by adding sliced almonds for ears, bits of black olives for eyes, and long slices of green onion for whiskers and tails. If any tea party guests have nut allergies, simply replace the almonds with thin, crosswise slices of celery.

1 (24-ounce) bag small red potatoes
2 tablespoons olive oil
1¾ teaspoons kosher salt, divided
½ cup finely grated sharp Cheddar cheese
6 tablespoons sour cream
1 tablespoon whole milk
24 (2½x⅛-inch) slices green onion, green parts only
24 (¾x⅛-inch) slices green onion, green parts only
48 almond slices, lightly toasted
2 black olives, finely chopped

• Preheat oven to 425°. Line a rimmed baking sheet with parchment paper.
• In a large bowl, toss potatoes with oil and 1 teaspoon salt. Place potatoes on prepared baking sheet.
• Bake until tender when pierced with a fork, approximately 18 minutes. Let cool on pan on a wire cooling rack.
• Reduce oven temperature to 375°.
• Using a sharp knife, cut 12 potatoes in half lengthwise.

Peel and discard skins from remaining potatoes. Transfer peeled potatoes to a medium bowl.
• Using a ¼ teaspoon, scoop a small well from potato halves, adding pulp from wells to bowl with whole, peeled potatoes. Using a fork, slightly mash whole, peeled potatoes. Add cheese, sour cream, and remaining ¾ teaspoon salt. Beat with a mixer at medium speed until smooth. Add milk, beating until incorporated (mixture will be thick). Transfer mixture to a piping bag fitted with an open-star tip (Wilton #4B).
• Pipe potato mixture back and forth into potato shells. Return filled potato shells to baking sheet.
• Bake until warmed through, 15 to 20 minutes. Let potatoes cool to room temperature.
• In a medium bowl full of cold water, place 2½-inch-long green onion slices to curl for tails. Blot dry on paper towels just before using.
• To create whiskers, using a sharp knife, gently cut a slit at each end of ¾-inch-long green onion slices.
• On each potato, gently press into place 2 almond slices for ears. Using tweezers, place 2 olive bits for eyes, green onion whiskers, and a green onion tail. Serve within an hour.

MAKE-AHEAD TIP: Potatoes can be prepared and filled up to 3 days ahead; let cool completely, place in an airtight container, and refrigerate. Up to 2 hours before serving, warm filled potatoes in a 375° oven. Let cool before decorating as mice.

Pumpkin Cupcakes
with Molasses Frosting

Makes approximately 12

Topped with cute animal-shaped sugar decorations, these moist cupcakes and rich buttercream truly capture a taste of autumn.

½ cup unsalted butter, softened
¾ cup firmly packed dark brown sugar
¼ cup granulated sugar
1 teaspoon vanilla extract
2 large eggs
1½ cups all-purpose flour
1 teaspoon pumpkin pie spice
1½ teaspoons baking powder
¼ teaspoon kosher salt
¾ cup canned pumpkin puree*
1 tablespoon whole milk
Molasses Frosting (recipe follows)
Garnish: animal-shaped sugar decorations**

• Preheat oven to 350°. Line a 12-well muffin pan with paper liners.
• In a large bowl, beat together butter, sugars, and vanilla extract with a mixer at medium speed until light and fluffy, stopping occasionally to scrape down sides of bowl. Add eggs, one at a time, beating well after each addition.
• In a small bowl, whisk together flour, pumpkin pie spice, baking powder, and salt.
• In another small bowl, whisk together pumpkin and milk. With mixer at low speed, beat flour mixture into butter mixture, alternating with pumpkin mixture, beginning and ending with flour mixture. Divide batter among wells of prepared muffin pan. Tap pan on counter twice.
• Bake until a wooden pick inserted in centers comes out clean, approximately 22 minutes. Let cool in pan for 5 minutes. Transfer cupcakes to a wire cooling rack and let cool completely.
• Place Molasses Frosting in a piping bag fitted with a large open star tip (Wilton #1M). Pipe a frosting rosette onto each cupcake.
• Garnish each with a sugar decoration, if desired. Carefully wrap cupcakes with decorative cupcake wrappers*, if desired.

Do not use pumpkin pie filling.
**We used Woodland Animals Sugar Decorations and Nest Cupcake Wrappers from Fancy Flours, fancyflours.com or 800-990-4510.*

Molasses Frosting

Makes approximately 1½ cups

A little molasses is all it takes to convert basic buttercream frosting into a memorable autumnal topping.

½ cup unsalted butter, softened
2½ cups confectioners' sugar
1 tablespoon whole milk
2 teaspoons molasses

• In a large bowl, beat butter with a mixer at medium speed until thick and creamy. Gradually add confectioners' sugar, milk, and molasses, beating until frosting is a spreadable consistency. Use immediately.

S'mores Pudding Cups

Makes approximately 12 servings

Made-from-scratch chocolate pudding evokes the campfire-favorite dessert s'mores with a topping of graham cracker pieces and mini marshmallows. Since these marshmallows are difficult to toast in the traditional manner due to their small size, we recommend using a handheld kitchen torch to brown them carefully as desired.

½ cup firmly packed dark brown sugar, divided
3 tablespoons cornstarch
1 large egg
1 large egg yolk
¼ teaspoon salt
2¼ cups whole milk
1 (4-ounce) bar bittersweet chocolate, finely chopped
2 tablespoons unsalted butter
1 teaspoon vanilla extract
Garnish: graham cracker pieces*, miniature
    marshmallows, and Autumn Leaves Wafer Paper**

• In a medium bowl, whisk together ¼ cup brown sugar, cornstarch, egg, egg yolk, and salt.
• In a medium saucepan, bring milk and remaining ¼ cup brown sugar to a simmer together over medium heat, stirring occasionally.
• Gradually add half of hot milk mixture to egg mixture, whisking well. Add egg mixture back to saucepan with remaining half of hot milk mixture, whisking until combined. Cook, stirring constantly, until mixture is thickened and bubbly, approximately 8 minutes. Remove from heat.
• Add chocolate, butter, and vanilla extract to saucepan, stirring until chocolate and butter melt and mixture is smooth. Spoon chocolate pudding into 12 small heatproof cups. Place a sheet of plastic wrap directly onto pudding surface to prevent a skin from forming. Refrigerate until cold and set, at least 3 hours.
• Just before serving, remove and discard plastic wrap. Garnish pudding with graham cracker pieces and several marshmallows. Using a handheld kitchen torch, lightly brown marshmallows, if desired. Top with an edible leaf, if desired.

For gluten-free pudding cups, garnish with gluten-free graham cracker pieces.
**We used Autumn Leaves Wafer Paper from Fancy Flours, fancyflours.com or 800-990-4510.*

Chocolate-Vanilla Pinwheels

Makes approximately 30 cookies

Dutch-process cocoa powder and roasted salted pistachios star in these eye-catching cookies that are intended to resemble crosswise sections of logs.

1 cup plus 2 tablespoons unsalted butter, softened
¾ cup confectioners' sugar
1½ teaspoons vanilla extract
1¾ cups plus 2 tablespoons all-purpose flour
½ teaspoon fine sea salt
1 large egg white
1½ tablespoons Dutch-process cocoa powder
⅔ cup finely chopped roasted salted pistachios

• Coat 4 (16x12-inch) parchment paper sheets with cooking spray.
• In a large bowl, beat butter with a mixer at medium speed until smooth. Add confectioners' sugar and vanilla extract, beating at medium speed until thick and creamy, approximately 2 minutes.
• In a small bowl, whisk together flour and salt. Add flour mixture and egg white to butter mixture, beating until just combined, scraping down sides of bowl as needed. Transfer half of dough (approximately 9 ounces) to a medium bowl and set aside. Add cocoa powder to remaining dough in bowl, beating until blended, scraping down sides of bowl as needed.
• Place vanilla dough on cooking spray side of a prepared parchment paper sheet, and cover with another parchment paper sheet, cooking spray side down. Using a rolling pin, roll out dough to a 12x6-inch rectangle, occasionally gently peeling back paper to straighten sides of dough. Repeat with chocolate dough and remaining 2 prepared parchment paper sheets. Refrigerate both doughs for approximately 1 hour. Let stand at room temperature until paper can be easily removed, approximately 15 minutes.
• Gently remove top sheet of paper from chocolate dough. Repeat with vanilla dough. Place vanilla dough, paper side up, on top of chocolate dough. Gently remove top sheet of paper. Starting with a long side, roll dough into a log, using bottom parchment to help roll. Roll dough log in pistachios. Place dough log on a sheet of plastic wrap, twisting ends to seal. Refrigerate until firm, approximately 1 hour.
• Preheat oven to 350°. Line 2 rimmed baking sheets with parchment paper.

- Using a sharp knife, trim and discard ½ inch from each end of log. Cut log into scant ½-inch thick slices. Place slices 1-inch apart on prepared baking sheets.
- Bake until set on tops and lightly browned on bottoms, approximately 16 minutes. Let cool on pans for 5 minutes. Transfer cookies to a wire rack and let cool completely. Store in an airtight container at room temperature.

AFTERNOON TEA FOR *Mermaids*

The
MENU

SCONE
Butterscotch Scones
Organic Butterfly Pea

SAVORIES
Veggie Sushi
Stuffed Pasta Shells
Cheesy Pinwheels
Organic Wizards Brew
(contains caffeine)

SWEETS
Honey-Vanilla Bean Madeleines
Mermaid Tail Treats
Citrus Mermaid Cake
with Marine Buttercream
Organic Strawberry Kisses

Tea Pairings by True Leaf Tea Company
346-701-7221 • trueleaftea.com

Mermaids will happily partake
of this sea-themed tea, boasting
accoutrements and fare that
echo the sandy shores and deep
blue waters of the ocean.

Butterscotch Scones
Makes approximately 12

Butterscotch chips dot the dough of these starfish-shaped scones that are sweetened with light brown sugar.

3 cups all-purpose flour
3 tablespoons firmly packed light brown sugar
4 teaspoons baking powder
½ teaspoon fine sea salt
½ cup cold unsalted butter, cubed
1⅓ cups plus 1 tablespoon cold heavy whipping cream, divided
½ cup butterscotch chips

• Preheat oven to 375°. Line a rimmed baking sheet with parchment paper.
• In a large bowl, whisk together flour, sugar, baking powder, and salt. Using a pastry blender or 2 forks, cut butter into flour mixture until it resembles coarse crumbs. Using a fork, stir in 1⅓ cups cream until a shaggy dough begins to come together. Working gently, bring mixture together with hands until a dough forms. (It is OK if a few dry bits remain.)
• Turn out dough onto a lightly floured surface, and knead gently until smooth by patting dough and folding it in half 4 to 5 times. Using a rolling pin, roll out dough to a ½-inch thickness. Scatter chips over half of dough. Fold other half of dough over chips to enclose them. Lightly roll out dough again to a ½-inch thickness. Using a 3¾-inch starfish-shaped or star-shaped cutter dipped in flour, cut as many scones as possible from dough, rerolling scraps once. Place scones 1 inch apart on prepared baking sheet. Freeze for 15 minutes.
• Brush tops of scones with remaining 1 tablespoon cream.
• Bake until scones are golden brown and a wooden pick inserted in centers comes out clean, approximately 15 minutes. Let cool on baking sheet for 5 minutes. Serve warm or at room temperature.

RECOMMENDED CONDIMENTS:
Clotted cream
Orange marmalade

Veggie Sushi

Makes 32 slices

Cucumber, avocado, and carrot fill the center of this sushi, which is made with traditional white rice and nori (seaweed) sheets. Although our version is vegetarian, you could certainly add seafood to the rolls, if desired.

1 English cucumber
2 sushi nori sheets, cut in half
1 avocado, halved and pitted
Sushi Rice (recipe follows)
⅔ cup coarsely grated carrot
Yum yum sauce (optional)
Soy sauce (optional)

• Wrap a bamboo sushi mat with plastic wrap.
• Trim ends from cucumber. Peel cucumber and cut lengthwise into quarters. Trim each quarter into ¼-inch-thick sticks and cut to width of nori sheets, discarding scraps.
• Cut each piece of avocado in half again. Peel avocado, then place cut side down on a cutting board, and cut into thin slices.
• Place a small bowl of cold water on workstation. Place a nori piece on prepared mat, shiny side down, with one long side closest to you. Using fingers, press a heaping ½ cup Sushi Rice in center of nori sheet. Dipping fingers in cold water as needed, use fingers as rakes to push and pull rice to cover nori sheet, leaving a ¼-inch border on one long side closest to you. (You should not see the nori through the rice.) Flip nori over, rice side down and with border still closest to you.
• Working with 1 nori sheet at a time, place approximately 2½ tablespoons carrot along bottom third of each nori sheet. Place a cucumber stick next to carrot. Top carrot with 4 avocado slices each, slightly overlapping as needed. Starting at border end, fold nori over ingredients completely, using your fingers to keep ingredients in place and using mat to help. Continue to roll up sushi tightly, pushing back on mat as you roll to help make sure it is tight. Run your hands along the roll to make sure it is even before removing mat. Using a wet sharp knife, cut each roll into 8 pieces. Serve with yum yum sauce or soy sauce, if desired.

MAKE-AHEAD TIP: Sliced sushi rolls can be placed in a single layer in an airtight container and refrigerated for a few hours until ready to serve.

Sushi Rice

Makes approximately 1¼ cups

To hold its shape, sushi requires sticky, short-grain rice, such as this, which is dressed with a mixture of rice vinegar and sugar.

1 cup sushi rice
1½ cups cold water, plus more for rinsing
2 tablespoons rice vinegar
2½ teaspoons granulated sugar
¼ teaspoon fine sea salt

• In a fine strainer, rinse rice with cold running water until water runs clear. Pour rice into a medium saucepan with 1½ cups cold water; let sit for 30 minutes.
• Bring rice to a boil over medium-high heat; immediately turn heat to low and cover tightly. Cook for 20 minutes. Remove from heat and let sit, covered, for 10 minutes.
• In a small microwavable bowl, heat together vinegar, sugar, and salt in a microwave oven in 15 second increments, stirring between each, until sugar dissolves. Pour evenly over rice and fold in gently with a wooden spoon to combine. Transfer rice mixture to a medium bowl, and let cool to room temperature, stirring occasionally. Use immediately.

salt. Gently fold in white balsamic vinegar reduction until evenly distributed. Divide salad mixture among prepared shells. Serve immediately, or place in a single layer in an airtight container and refrigerate until ready to serve within a few hours.

While only 9 pasta shells are needed, we recommend cooking at least 12 in case any shells split during the cooking process.
**We used Alessi.*

Cheesy Pinwheels
Makes approximately 19

Two types of cheese encased in puff pastry make these savory treats virtually irresistible, especially when served warm.

1 large egg
2 teaspoons water
¼ teaspoon fine sea salt
½ cup grated Gruyère cheese
¼ cup grated Parmesan cheese
½ (17.3-ounce) package frozen puff pastry (1 sheet), thawed

• Preheat oven to 400°. Line a rimmed baking sheet with parchment paper.
• In a small bowl, whisk together egg, 2 teaspoons water, and salt to make an egg wash.
• In another small bowl, stir together cheeses.
• On a lightly floured surface, unroll pastry sheet. Brush sheet with egg wash. Top with cheese mixture, leaving a ½-inch border on one short end. Starting on opposite short end, roll up, jellyroll style to encase cheeses. Wrap in plastic wrap, and freeze until slightly firm, approximately 15 minutes.
• Remove plastic wrap, and place pastry log on a cutting board. Roll pastry log back and forth to make sure it's even and round. Using a serrated bread knife in a sawing motion, trim ends of pastry log and cut into ½-inch-thick slices. Place slices, cut side down, at least 1 inch apart on prepared baking sheet.
• Brush tops of slices with egg wash.
• Bake until lightly golden brown, approximately 15 minutes. Rotate pan, reduce oven temperature to 350°, and continue to bake until dough looks dry and golden brown, approximately 5 minutes more. Let cool on pan for 5 minutes. Serve warm or at room temperature.

Stuffed Pasta Shells
Makes 9

Jumbo pasta shells are a fun way to present a colorful salad for a marine-themed teatime.

1⅝ teaspoon fine sea salt, divided
9 jumbo pasta shells*
2 cups chopped green leaf lettuce
6 mini mozzarella cheese pearls, quartered
¼ cup quartered multicolor grape tomatoes
¼ cup very thinly sliced red cabbage
⅛ teaspoon ground black pepper
1 tablespoon white balsamic vinegar reduction**

• Bring a medium saucepan filled three-fourths with water to a boil over high heat. Stir in 1½ teaspoons salt. Add pasta, and cook, stirring occasionally, until al dente, 12 to 14 minutes (or according to package directions). Drain, and rinse under cold water until chilled, letting excess water drip off.
• In a medium bowl, stir together lettuce, cheese, tomatoes, cabbage, pepper, and remaining ⅛ teaspoon

Honey–Vanilla Bean Madeleines
Makes 14

Madeleines are classic French sweets that are baked in pans with iconic shell-shaped wells. Garnish them with sparkling sugar as we have here, or for a simpler look, dust lightly with confectioners' sugar.

½ cup all-purpose flour
⅓ cup granulated sugar
½ teaspoon baking powder
¼ teaspoon fine sea salt
½ cup unsalted butter, melted, plus more for brushing
2 large eggs, room temperature
1 tablespoon orange blossom honey
1 tablespoon vanilla bean paste
1 cup confectioners' sugar
4 teaspoons whole milk
½ cup multicolored sparkling sugar*

• Preheat oven to 350°. Brush 14 wells of a 16-well madeleine pan with melted butter.
• In a medium bowl, whisk together flour, sugar, baking powder, and salt.
• In another medium bowl, whisk together ½ cup melted butter, eggs, honey, and vanilla bean paste. Gradually whisk butter mixture into flour mixture until combined and smooth. Spoon 1½ tablespoons into each prepared well of pan.
• Bake until madeleines are puffed and golden, 8 to 10 minutes. Let cool in pan for 5 minutes. Remove from pan, and let cool completely on wire racks.
• In a medium bowl, whisk together confectioners' sugar and milk until smooth (mixture will be thick). Place sparkling sugar in a small bowl. Working with one madeleine at a time, carefully dip just the edges of madeleine into the glaze and then immediately dip glazed edges into sparkling sugar to coat. Place on serving platter, shell side up, and let glaze set before serving, approximately 10 minutes.

*We used Sweet Tooth Fairy® Crystal Sugar from Michaels, michaels.com.

EDITOR'S NOTE: If you only have a 12-well pan, bake in batches, letting batter sit at room temperature and brushing pan with butter again before baking the second batch.

Mermaid Tail Treats

Makes 12

Cereal treats shaped like mermaid tails add a fun element to this afternoon tea. Children will enjoy helping make this recipe, but adult supervision is recommended.

5 tablespoons unsalted butter
¼ teaspoon fine sea salt
4 cups mini marshmallows
½ teaspoon vanilla extract
4 cups crisp rice cereal
2 cups fruit-flavored crisp rice cereal
Blue vanilla-flavored melting wafers*, melted
   according to package directions

• Place 2 large parchment paper pieces on the counter. Spray with cooking spray.
• In a large saucepan, melt together butter and salt over medium heat. Cook, stirring constantly, until mixture is golden brown and has a nutty aroma, 3 to 4 minutes. Immediately stir in marshmallows; reduce heat to medium-low, stirring constantly until marshmallows melt. Stir in vanilla extract. Remove from heat. Stir in cereals until evenly coated.
• Using a spatula, spoon mixture onto a prepared parchment paper piece. Top with remaining prepared parchment paper piece, sprayed side down. Using hands, press mixture to a ¾-inch thickness. Remove top parchment and press in on edges of mixture to make sure they are even. Let cool completely at room temperature.
• Using a 3½-inch mermaid tail cookie cutter**, firmly press cookie cutter into cooled mixture and cut 12 shapes, discarding scraps.
• Dip top of tails into melted wafers, letting some excess drip off. Place vertically on a clean piece of parchment paper, fins up, pressing down to make sure tails are stable, straight, and even. Let sit in a cool, dry place until melting wafers harden. Store in an airtight container.

We used Sweet Tooth Fairy® Meltables from Michaels, michaels.com. Make sure to stir melting wafers well after melting so separation does not occur while cooling.

**We used a Celebrate It Mermaid Tail Cutter from Michaels, michaels.com. There is no need to spray cookie cutter before using.*

Citrus Mermaid Cake

Makes 8 to 12 servings

Tangy cake layers flavored with fresh lemon and orange hide beneath a sea of rich buttercream for a decadent finish to our mermaid-themed teatime.

½ cup unsalted butter, softened
3 tablespoons neutral oil
1⅓ cups granulated sugar
1 tablespoon fresh lemon zest
1 tablespoon fresh orange zest
3 large eggs, room temperature
1 teaspoon vanilla extract
2 cups unbleached cake flour
1¼ teaspoons baking powder
¼ teaspoon fine sea salt
½ cup sour cream, room temperature
¼ cup fresh orange juice
Marine Buttercream (recipe follows)
Garnish: edible pearl spray* and sprinkles**

• Preheat oven to 325°. Line bottoms of 2 (8-inch) round cake pans with parchment paper and spray with baking spray with flour.
• In a large bowl, beat together butter and oil at medium speed with a mixer until combined and smooth. Beat in sugar and zests at medium speed until fluffy, 3 to 4 minutes, stopping to scrape down sides of bowl. Add eggs, one at a time, beating well after each addition. Beat in vanilla extract.
• In a medium bowl, whisk together flour, baking powder, and salt. Gradually add flour mixture to butter mixture alternately with sour cream and orange juice, beginning and ending with flour mixture, beating just until combined after each addition, scraping down sides of bowl as needed. Divide batter evenly between prepared pans, smoothing tops.
• Bake until a wooden pick inserted in centers comes out clean, 25 to 30 minutes. Let cool in pans for 10 minutes. Remove from pans, and let cool completely on wire racks.
• Place one cake layer on cake plate. Spread 1½ cups Marine Buttercream on top of cake. Top with remaining cake layer. Spread a very thin layer of buttercream on top and sides of cake. Place remaining buttercream in a piping bag fitted with a medium round tip (Ateco #808). Starting at the bottom edge of the cake, pipe a single row of dots completely around the cake, pulling piping

tip up as you finish piping the dot, or taking a mini offset spatula, placing it in the center of the dot, and swiping up. Pipe a second row, offset from first row, repeating pulling or swiping technique until sides of cake are covered. Starting on outside edge of top of cake and ending at center, repeat pattern on top of cake, pulling piping tip or swiping spatula toward center of cake. If an iridescent look is desired, spray cake with edible pearl spray. Garnish with sprinkles, if desired. Cover and refrigerate for at least 1 hour to set buttercream.

We used Wilton Color Mist in Pearl.
**We used Sweet Tooth Fairy® Mermazing Sprinkle Mix from Michaels, michaels.com.*

Marine Buttercream

Makes approximately 6 cups

A basic buttercream is transformed with three colors of gel food coloring to get just the right hue to evoke images of the ocean.

2 cups unsalted butter, softened
¼ teaspoon fine sea salt
1 (2-pound) bag confectioners' sugar
½ cup cold heavy whipping cream
2 teaspoons vanilla extract
Teal, green, and blue gel food coloring*

• In a large bowl, beat together butter and salt at low speed with a mixer until smooth. Gradually add confectioners' sugar (approximately 1 cup at a time), alternating with cream (approximately 1 tablespoon at a time), beating until smooth. Continue adding confectioners' sugar and cream in this manner until fully combined. Increase mixer speed to medium, and beat until smooth and fluffy, approximately 1 minute. Beat in vanilla extract.
• In a small bowl, place 2 cups buttercream. Fold in enough teal food coloring to achieve desired marine hue.
• In another small bowl, place 1 cup buttercream. Fold in enough green food coloring to achieve desired marine hue.
• To remaining buttercream, fold in enough blue food coloring to achieve desired marine hue. Add teal and green buttercreams, swirling colors together once. Use immediately.

We used Wilton Teal, Leaf Green, and Sky Blue.

RAINBOWS &
Unicorns

The
MENU

SCONE
Five-Flavor Scones
Organic Strawberry
Lemon Twist Herbal Tea

SAVORIES
Unicorn Sandwiches
Fruity Yogurt Parfaits
Ribbon Rainbow Sandwiches
Organic Autumn Mist Herbal Tea

SWEETS
Vanilla-Almond Pinwheel Cookies
Dreamy Candy Bark
Strawberry Unicorn Cupcakes
Solstice Moon Herbal Tea

Tea Pairings by The Boulder Tea Company
303-817-7057 • boulderteaco.com

A dreamy, multicolored palette and an array of unicorn-shaped treats create an extraordinary setting for tea and giggles to be shared.

Five-Flavor Scones

Makes 16

Five—yes, five—extracts impart fruity and nutty notes to this scone, which also incorporates two types of flour for best texture. Topped with whipped cream and coconut dyed to match the party décor, these wedge-shaped scones are sure to serve as tasty odes to the unicorn's horn.

1½ cups all-purpose flour*
1 cup cake flour*
⅓ cup granulated sugar
1 tablespoon baking powder
½ teaspoon fine sea salt
5 tablespoons cold unsalted butter, cubed
½ cup plus 2 tablespoons cold heavy whipping cream, divided
2 large eggs, divided
¼ teaspoon vanilla extract
¼ teaspoon almond extract
¼ teaspoon lemon extract
¼ teaspoon orange extract
¼ teaspoon coconut extract
Garnish: Sweetened Whipped Cream and
    Dyed Coconut (recipes follow)

• Preheat oven to 375°. Line a rimmed baking sheet with parchment paper.
• In a large bowl, whisk together both flours, sugar, baking powder, and salt. Using a pastry blender or 2 forks, cut butter into flour mixture until it resembles coarse crumbs.
• In a small bowl, whisk together ½ cup plus 1 tablespoon cream, 1 egg, and 5 extracts. Add to flour mixture, stirring just until ingredients are combined and a shaggy dough begins to form. Working gently, bring mixture together with hands until a dough forms. (Dough will be firm once it comes together.)
• Turn dough out onto a lightly floured surface, and knead gently until smooth by patting dough and folding it in half 4 to 5 times. Divide dough into 2 equal portions. Using a rolling pin, roll out each portion of dough to a ¾-inch-thick round. (Each portion should measure approximately 5 inches in diameter.) Pat edges of dough rounds to neaten and smooth. Using a long sharp knife, cut each circle into 8 equal wedges. Place scones 2 inches apart on prepared baking sheet. Freeze for 15 minutes.

• In a small bowl, whisk together remaining egg and remaining 1 tablespoon cream. Brush tops of scones with egg mixture.
• Bake until edges of scones are golden brown and a wooden pick inserted in centers comes out clean, 18 to 20 minutes. Let cool completely before garnishing.
• Just before serving scones, place Sweetened Whipped Cream in a piping bag fitted with a large open star tip (Wilton #1M). Pipe rows of whipped cream horizontally across each cooled scone. Sprinkle each row with a different color of Dyed Coconut. Serve immediately.

Spoon flour into measuring cup without packing and then scrape off excess with a straight edge to level.

Sweetened Whipped Cream

Makes 2 cups

What better topping for a scone than fluffy whipped cream that is slightly sweet? For variety, the vanilla extract can be easily switched out for one of the other extract flavors used in our Five-Flavor Scones.

1 cup cold heavy whipping cream
2 tablespoons confectioners' sugar
½ teaspoon vanilla extract

• In a deep bowl, beat together cream, confectioners' sugar, and vanilla extract at high speed with a mixer until thickened and soft peaks form. Use immediately.

Dyed Coconut

Makes 3 cups

Tinting coconut couldn't be easier than this no-bake method. While we used red, green, and yellow for our Five-Flavor Scones' garnish, we recommend selecting hues that will match those of the party's theme. For best results, dye the coconut a few days before it will be used.

3 cups sweetened flaked coconut, divided
Red liquid food coloring
Green liquid food coloring
Yellow liquid food coloring

• Line 3 rimmed baking sheets with wax paper.
• Place 1 cup coconut each in 3 resealable plastic bags.
• To one bag, add a very small amount of red food

coloring. To another bag, add a very small amount of green food coloring. To remaining bag, add a very small amount of yellow food coloring. Close bags and move coconut around by shaking and massaging bags to evenly distribute color onto coconut. Pour dyed coconut onto prepared baking sheets, spreading into an even layer, keeping colors separated. Let coconut dry at room temperature for several hours. Once coconut is dry, store in resealable plastic bags or airtight containers until needed. Use within 5 days.

Unicorn Sandwiches

Makes 12

These cute ham, cheese, and turkey sandwiches are sure to be hits with children of all ages. To keep from compressing the edges of the bread when cutting out the unicorn shapes, be sure the bread is completely frozen.

24 slices firm white sandwich bread, frozen
12 thin slices deli-style oven-roasted turkey
12 thin slices deli-style cooked ham
12 thin slices deli-style yellow American cheese
½ cup mayonnaise
2 teaspoons prepared yellow mustard
Garnish: black decorating gel*

• Using an approximately 3-inch unicorn-shaped cutter**, cut 24 shapes from frozen bread, discarding scraps. To prevent bread from drying out, cover with damp paper towels or place in a resealable plastic bag, and let thaw at room temperature.

• Using the same cutter, cut 12 shapes each from turkey, ham, and cheese, discarding scraps.

• In a small bowl, stir together mayonnaise and mustard to combine. Spread onto each bread unicorn, making sure that 12 bread unicorns face left and the remaining 12 face right so that shapes will match when combined as a sandwich. On spread side of each left-facing bread unicorn, layer a cheese unicorn, a ham unicorn, and a turkey unicorn, and cover each with a right-facing bread unicorn, spread side down. Serve immediately, or cover with damp paper towels, place in a single layer in an airtight container, and refrigerate for a few hours until ready to serve.

• Just before serving, squeeze black writing gel into a small piping bag, and cut a tiny hole in tip. Draw a closed eye with lashes onto each sandwich. Serve immediately.

*We used Betty Crocker black writing gel.
**We used a Sunny Side Up Bakery unicorn metal cookie cutter from Hobby Lobby, available at hobbylobby.com.

"Always be yourself, unless you can be a unicorn. Then always be a unicorn."

—ELLE LOTHLORIEN

Fruity Yogurt Parfaits
Makes 12 (4-ounce) servings

Cheery fresh-fruit parfaits are perfect for this tea party and can be mostly assembled ahead of time. Be sure to add the cereal to the glasses only right before serving, or the crisp rice will become soggy.

1½ cups chopped fresh orange segments
3 cups vanilla-flavored Greek yogurt, divided
1½ cups chopped fresh kiwi
1 cup fruit-flavored crisp rice cereal
12 thin slices unpeeled star fruit

• In 12 (4-ounce) glasses, arrange orange in an even layer. Place a layer of yogurt on top of orange segments. Divide 1½ cups yogurt, kiwi, and remaining 1½ cups yogurt among glasses in even layers. At this point, parfaits can be stored in the refrigerator for up to an hour before serving.
• Just before serving, top parfaits with an even layer of cereal. Insert a wooden pick into edge of each star fruit slice, and place pick ends into parfaits. (IMPORTANT: To avoid choking on the picks, children should be supervised when eating parfaits.)

Ribbon Rainbow Sandwiches
Makes 12

Colorful vegetables give these triple-stack tea sandwiches their rainbow-like look. The bread is spread with a generous amount of ranch-flavored cream cheese, which might persuade even the pickiest of eaters to give these savories a try.

Ranch Cream Cheese Spread (recipe follows)
12 very thin slices whole-wheat bread, divided
½ cup very finely chopped red cabbage*
½ cup stem-free baby spinach leaves, divided
½ cup very finely chopped carrot*

• Spread a thin, even layer of Ranch Cream Cheese Spread onto 8 bread slices. Spread a thin, even layer of Ranch Cream Cheese Spread onto both sides of remaining 4 bread slices.

• On spread side of 4 bread slices, arrange approximately 2 tablespoons each chopped cabbage. Arrange half of spinach leaves over cabbage. Top with each with a bread slice that has spread on both sides. Arrange approximately 2 tablespoons each chopped carrot over spread layer. Arrange remaining half of spinach leaves over carrot. Cover with remaining bread slices, spread side down to create 4 triple-stack sandwiches.
• Using a thin, serrated bread knife in a gentle, sawing motion, trim and discard crusts evenly from all sandwiches. Cut each sandwich into 3 equal rectangles. Serve immediately, or cover with damp paper towels, place in an airtight container, refrigerate, and serve within an hour.

*We used a small food processor to finely chop vegetables.

Ranch Cream Cheese Spread
Makes 1¼ cups

Laced with a trio of fresh herbs, this savory cream cheese spread also gets rich taste and texture from mayonnaise and sour cream.

1 (8-ounce) package cream cheese, softened
2 tablespoons mayonnaise
2 tablespoons sour cream
¼ teaspoon garlic powder
¼ teaspoon onion powder
¼ teaspoon fine sea salt
⅛ teaspoon ground black pepper
1 tablespoon finely chopped fresh dill
1 tablespoon finely chopped flat-leaf parsley
1 tablespoon finely chopped green onion
   (green tops only)

• In a medium bowl, vigorously stir together cream cheese, mayonnaise, sour cream, garlic powder, onion powder, salt, and pepper until well combined and creamy. Stir in dill, parsley, and green onion until incorporated. Use immediately, or cover, refrigerate, and use within a day.

Vanilla-Almond Pinwheel Cookies

Makes approximately 36

Flavored with vanilla and almond and garnished with sanding sugar, these pinwheel cookies are bound to impress guests. We used yellow and violet gel food coloring to tint the doughs, but you can select other colors to suit the décor.

1 cup unsalted butter, softened
1 cup granulated sugar
1 large egg
½ teaspoon vanilla extract
¼ teaspoon almond extract
3 cups all-purpose flour
1½ teaspoons baking powder
½ teaspoon fine sea salt
Lemon yellow gel food coloring
Violet gel food coloring
Garnish: light purple sanding sugar*

• Preheat oven to 350°. Line 2 rimmed baking sheets with parchment paper.

• In a large bowl, beat together butter and sugar at high speed with a mixer until light and creamy, approximately 3 minutes. Beat in egg and extracts until incorporated. Scrape down sides of bowl.

• In a medium bowl, whisk together flour, baking powder, and salt. Add to flour mixture, beating at medium-low speed until combined and scraping down sides of bowl as needed. Divide dough into 2 equal portions.

• Return one dough portion to mixing bowl, and beat in enough yellow food coloring to achieve desired hue. Remove dough to a lightly floured sheet of wax paper. Repeat process to tint remaining dough portion violet, placing it on a separate sheet of wax paper.

• Using a lightly floured rolling pin, roll out each dough portion ⅛-inch thick into a 15x9½-inch rectangle. Transfer dough with wax paper to baking sheets, and place in freezer just long enough to chill dough, being careful not to let dough freeze completely.

• When dough is chilled, remove wax paper from yellow dough and place dough on a lightly floured surface. Remove wax paper from violet dough and place dough on top of yellow dough. Using a knife, trim dough stack as necessary to line up edges so that rectangle is neatly shaped. Roll up doughs together firmly and evenly, beginning at a short end, so that spiral will be uniform inside. (Use a bench scraper to help lift dough from surface and maintain an even roll.)

• On another sheet of wax paper, heavily sprinkle sanding sugar. Roll dough log in sugar, pressing lightly for sugar to adhere. Wrap dough log with another sheet of wax paper and place on a rimmed baking sheet. Place in freezer for 15 minutes.

• Remove wax paper and place dough log on a cutting surface. Using a sharp knife, and pressing downward instead of sawing, cut ¼-inch-thick crosswise slices from dough log. Coat edges of cookies in additional sanding sugar, if desired. Place cookies 2 inches apart on prepared baking sheets.

• Bake until edges and bottoms of cookies are very light golden brown, 8 to 10 minutes. Remove cookies to wire racks and let cool completely. Store cookies in an airtight container for up to 3 days or freeze for longer storage in an airtight container with layers separated by wax paper.

*We used Sunny Side Up Bakery Lavender Sanding Sugar from Hobby Lobby, hobbylobby.com.

Dreamy Candy Bark
Makes ¾ pound

Fanciful edible sprinkles decorate a simple candy bark made from melting wafers. Since a microwave oven is the only appliance required, children will enjoy making this with adult supervision.

1 (10-ounce) package white vanilla-flavored melting
   wafers*
Edible cake glitter**
Edible confetti sprinkles**
Edible wafer flower sprinkles**

• Line a rimmed baking sheet with a silicone nonstick baking mat.

• Melt wafers according to package directions. Using an offset spatula, spread melted wafers onto prepared baking sheet in a mostly even layer with some ripples for interest. Working quickly before melted wafers cool and begin to harden, sprinkle with desired amount of edible glitter, sprinkles, and wafer flowers.
• Place baking sheet in freezer to chill and harden candy quickly. Once candy is hardened, break into irregular pieces. Store in a covered container with layers separated by wax paper at room temperature or in the refrigerator if room is warm.

*We used Ghirardelli.
**We used Sunny Side Up Bakery light pink, purple, and gold Cake Glitter; ChocoMaker Shimmer Confetti Sprinkles; and Sunny Side Up Bakery Wafer Mini Flower Mix sprinkles from Hobby Lobby, hobbylobby.com.

Strawberry Unicorn Cupcakes

Makes 32

Partygoers might very well swoon over these charming unicorn cupcakes, which are just as delicious as they are attractive, with edible marshmallow "ears" and fruit leather "horns."

¼ cup unsalted butter, softened
½ cup granulated sugar
¼ cup seedless strawberry jam
1 large egg
¼ teaspoon vanilla extract
Red food coloring
1 cup cake flour
½ teaspoon baking powder
¼ teaspoon fine sea salt
⅛ teaspoon baking soda
2½ tablespoons whole buttermilk
Strawberry–Cream Cheese Frosting (recipe follows)
Garnish: decorative sparkling sugar*, marshmallow
    ears**, and strawberry fruit leather horns**

• Preheat oven to 350°.
• Line 32 wells of 2 (24-well) mini muffin pans with mini baking cups.
• In a large bowl, beat together butter and sugar at high speed with a mixer until light and fluffy, approximately 2 minutes. Beat in jam and egg until incorporated. Scrape down sides of bowl as needed. Beat in vanilla extract and enough food coloring to achieve desired hue.

• In a medium bowl, whisk together flour, baking powder, salt, and baking soda. With mixer at low speed, add to butter mixture, alternately with buttermilk, beginning and ending with flour mixture, beating until combined. Using a 2-teaspoon levered scoop, drop batter into prepared wells of muffin pans. (Don't overfill, or cupcakes will spill over.) Tap pans on countertop to level batter.
• Bake on middle rack of oven until a wooden pick inserted in centers comes out clean, 10 to 11 minutes. (Don't overbake, or cupcakes will be dry.) Remove cupcakes to a wire cooling rack, and let cool completely.
• Place Strawberry–Cream Cheese Frosting in a piping bag fitted with a large open star tip (Wilton #1M). Referring to how-to photographs on page 132, pipe a decorative swirl of frosting on top of each cupcake. Cupcakes can be stored in an airtight container in the refrigerator for up to a day in advance.
• Just before serving, garnish cupcakes with a sprinkle of sparkling sugar, 2 marshmallow ears each, and a fruit leather horn each, if desired.

*We used Sunny Side Up Bakery Edible Glitter & Sugar Blend from Hobby Lobby, hobbylobby.com.
**We used miniature marshmallows and Betty Crocker Fruit by the Foot. Turn to page 132 for how-to photographs and instructions for garnishes.

Strawberry–Cream Cheese Frosting

Makes 2½ cups

Strawberry-flavored cream cheese frosting is an ideal complement to our Strawberry Unicorn Cupcakes but would be equally good on basic vanilla cupcakes, too.

½ cup unsalted butter, softened
2 ounces cream cheese, softened
¼ teaspoon fine sea salt
3½ cups confectioners' sugar
3 tablespoons heavy whipping cream
2 teaspoons strawberry extract
¼ teaspoon vanilla extract
Pink gel food color

• In a large bowl, beat together butter, cream cheese, and salt at high speed with a mixer until combined. Beat in confectioners' sugar, heavy cream, and extracts, beginning at low speed and increasing to high speed, until frosting is light and fluffy, approximately 2 minutes. Beat in enough food coloring to achieve desired hue. Use immediately.

How-tos

Let these step-by-step photos serve as your visual guide
while you create these impressive and delicious teatime treats.

DRESSY CUCUMBER CANAPÉS
from page 22

1

Spread a thin, even layer of cream cheese
mixture onto each bread shape.

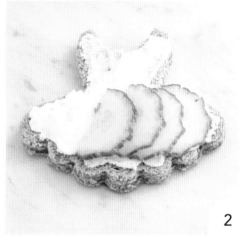

2

Shingle 7 cucumber pieces over tutu area of
each bread shape.

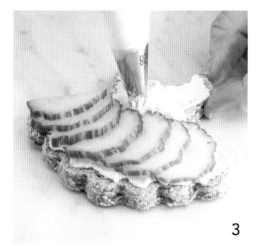

3

With a piping bag fitted with a French star tip
(Wilton #28), pipe a "belt" of cream cheese
mixture just above shingled cucumbers.

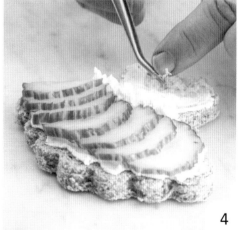

4

Just before serving, use tweezers to garnish
each canapé with lemon zest along neckline
area of leotard, if desired.

POINTE SHOE TEA SANDWICHES

from page 24

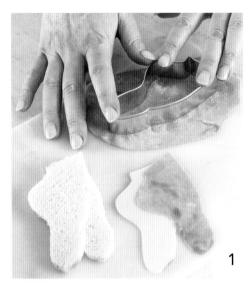

Using a 4¼-inch pointe shoe–shaped cutter, cut shapes from frozen bread, cheese, and ham.

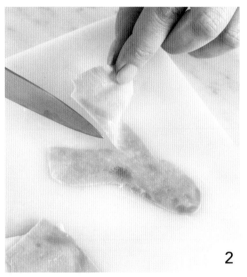

Using a paring knife, cut 12 ham shapes to fit onto the "shoe" portion of the sandwiches.

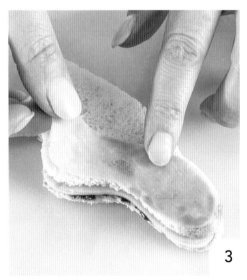

Place a ham "shoe" shape on top of each sandwich.

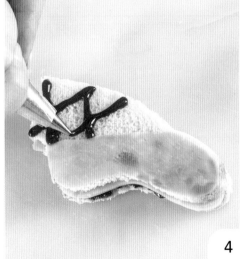

Pipe raspberry preserves in crisscrossing lines to look like the ribbons of a pointe shoe.

STRAWBERRY POINTE SHOES

from page 25

Dip each strawberry into melted wafers, leaving a small amount of berry showing at the top. Let set.

Carefully dip side of strawberry in pink melted wafer mixture.

Carefully dip opposite side of strawberry, leaving a triangle of white exposed in center.

Allow extra pink mixture to drip back into bowl before placing strawberry on parchment paper to set.

Transfer remaining pink mixture to a small piping bag and cut a ⅛-inch hole in tip.

Pipe crisscrossing lines over the exposed white area, connecting the 2 pink sides.

Continue piping to create the ribbons of a shoe. Refrigerate until set.

PAVLOVAS
from Blackberry Mini Pavlovas, page 27

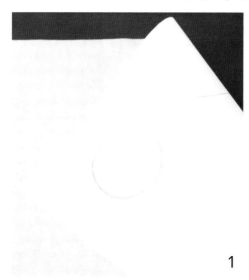

1

Using a pencil, draw 10 (2-inch) circles onto parchment paper; turn parchment over.

2

Working from the center outward, pipe concentric circles of meringue until circle is filled.

3

Pipe 1 to 2 extra layers onto perimeter of round to form a rim around the edge of meringue circle.

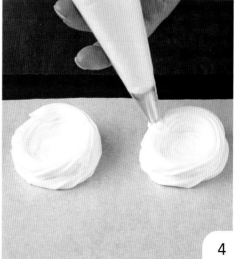

4

Repeat piping procedure to fill all traced circles. Bake according to recipe.

CLOWN CANAPÉS

from page 37

1

With piping tip perpendicular to cracker, pipe a ruffled dollop of cream cheese onto cracker.

2

Sprinkle with seasoning blend.

3

Place a tomato onto cream cheese on cracker, blossom end down, pressing down slightly to adhere.

4

Pipe another cream cheese dollop onto top of tomato.

5

Top with a corn snack. Arrange grated carrot as desired on cream cheese at base of corn snack.

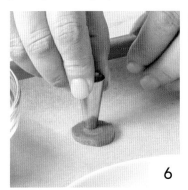

6

Using a small round piping tip as a cutter, cut circle from carrot slice.

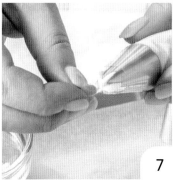

7

Using a small amount of cream cheese, adhere carrot circle to tomato for nose.

8

Serve immediately, or refrigerate for up to an hour before serving.

CUCUMBER BUTTERFLIES

from Lemon-Dill Cucumber Butterflies, page 50

Cut 12 (1-inch) pieces from a celery stalk with a slightly wide groove.

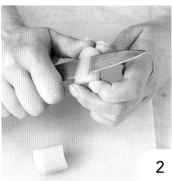

Cut a lengthwise portion from bottom of each celery piece to make them sit flat.

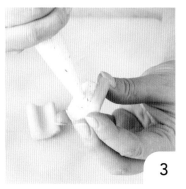

Pipe approximately 1 teaspoon cream cheese mixture into each celery piece.

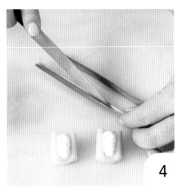

Cut green onion lengthwise into 1/16-inch-wide strips.

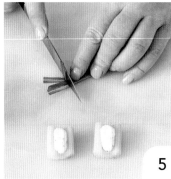

Cut green onion strips into 1-inch-long pieces.

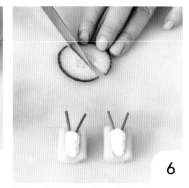

Insert 2 green onion pieces at one end of cream cheese mixture to create antennae.

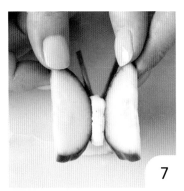

Press 2 cucumber slice halves, rounded edges together, into cream cheese mixture.

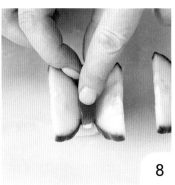

Cover cream cheese mixture with a pimiento strip.

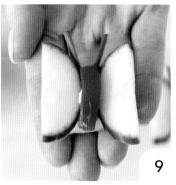

Serve immediately, or loosely cover and refrigerate for up to 30 minutes.

SUGARED ROSE PETALS

from Butterfly Rose & Lemon Shortbread, page 54

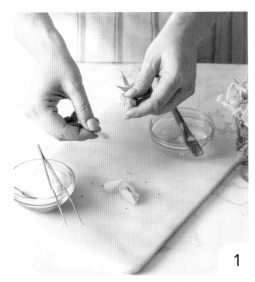

1

Gently remove and separate petals from pesticide-free spray roses.

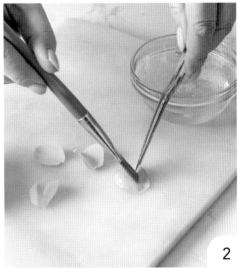

2

Using tweezers to hold each petal, brush egg wash over both sides of petal.

3

While holding petal with tweezers, sprinkle petal generously with sugar.

4

Place sugared petals on prepared baking sheet. Let dry overnight.

PIÑATA SUGAR COOKIES

from page 83

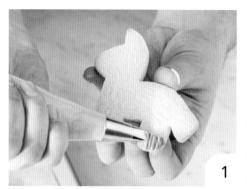

1

Starting at the bottom of each cookie, with narrow point of piping tip facing toward the piñata head, pipe tight "U" shapes to create a ruffled line.

2

Using a different icing color, pipe another ruffled line across cookie, slightly overlapping onto previous royal icing color.

3

Repeat piping procedure with remaining royal icing colors, slightly overlapping onto previous royal icing color.

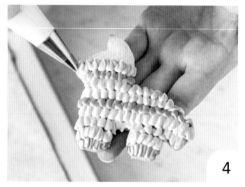

4

Use icing colors randomly or in the same order.

5

Repeat as needed until cookies are completely covered with icing.

6

Let cookies dry completely, 2 to 3 hours, before serving.

UNICORN CUPCAKES

from Strawberry Unicorn Cupcakes, page 121

Pipe a decorative swirl of frosting on top of each cupcake.

Garnish cupcakes with a sprinkle of sparkling sugar, if desired.

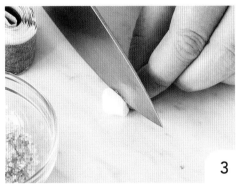

Using a sharp knife or kitchen scissors, cut mini marshmallows in half lengthwise.

Place 2 marshmallow ears per cupcake into top of frosting.

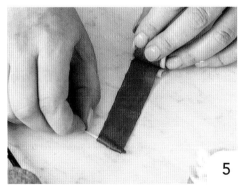

Place a wooden pick at an end of a 3-inch-long fruit leather piece. Roll up fruit leather in a spiral around pick to make a horn shape. Pinch end to seal. Remove pick. Let dry slightly.

Insert a fruit leather horn into top of frosting. Serve immediately.

Acknowledgments

EDITOR Lorna Reeves
ART DIRECTOR Leighann Lott Bryant
ASSOCIATE EDITOR Katherine Ellis
SENIOR COPY EDITOR Rhonda Lee Lother
EDITORIAL ASSISTANT Shelby Duffy
SENIOR DIGITAL IMAGE SPECIALIST
Delisa McDaniel
DIGITAL IMAGE SPECIALIST Clark Densmore

COVER

Photography by John O'Hagan
Styling by Courtni Bodiford
*Recipe Development by Kathleen Kanen and
Vanessa Rocchio • Food Styling by Kathleen Kanen*
Royal Albert *Friendship* teapot; Royal Albert
Gratitude footed cup and saucer set, 3-tiered tray,
salad plate, and tidbit plate; Royal Albert *Bridesmaid*
mini open sugar bowl and tray; International
Silver *Garland* spoon from Replacements, Ltd.,
800-737-5223, *replacements.com*. Tablecloth and
eyelet overlay from HomeGoods, 833-888-0776,
homegoods.com. Butterfly wands from Amazon,
amazon.com.

TEATIME FOR BALLERINAS

Photography by John O'Hagan
Styling by Courtni Bodiford
*Recipe Development by Becca Cummins and
Izzie Turner • Food Styling by Kathleen Kanen*
Pages 15–28: Zealax *Ballet* teapot and teacup
and saucer set; ballet bar and pointe shoes from
Amazon, *amazon.com*. Lenox *Petite Suite* luncheon
plate, creamer, covered sugar bowl, rectangular
tray; Reed & Barton *Ribbon Crest* butter spreader,
teaspoon, and salad fork; Arabia of Finland *Ribbons*
round platter; Ceralene *Romantique* cake plate,
handled cake plate, and medium cachepot from
Replacements, Ltd., 800-737-5223, *replacements
.com*. White tablecloth from Sferra, 732-225-6290,
sferra.com. *Lotus Bloom* napkins from Fox and
Brindle, *foxandbrindle.com*. *Sausalito* wallpaper
from French Market Collection, 985-646-0678,
frenchmarketcollection.com.

UNDER THE BIG TOP

Photography by John O'Hagan
Styling by Dorothy Walton
Recipe Development by Janet Lambert
Food Styling by Kathleen Kanen
Pages 29–42: Grace's Teaware *Josephine Red* salad
plate, flat cup and saucer set, creamer, covered
sugar bowl, and 2-tiered serving tray; Lenox *Larabee
Road* bread and butter plate; Royal Albert *Polka
Rose* 2-tiered stand and salad plate; Fitz & Floyd
Red Dotted Swiss round platter; Anna Weatherley
Simply Anna Polka round platter; Gorham *Fairfax*
butter spreader, salad fork, teaspoon, and sugar
tongs; Oneida *Patrick Henry* demitasse spoon from
Replacements, Ltd., 800-737-5223, *replacements
.com*. Sadler *Edwardian Entertainments Circus* teapot
from private collection. Appetizer platter from
Emile Henry, 302-326-4800, *emilehenryusa.com*.
Pudding cup from Pier 1, 800-245-4595, *pier1.com*.
Wicker giraffe planter from Hibiscus House, 407-
927-6080, *shophibiscushouse.com*. Meri Meri spots
and stripes party hats from Burke Décor, 888-338-
8111, *burkedecor.com*. Striped curtains from Target,
800-591-3869, *target.com*. Decorative pinwheels,
tassel steamers, and tickets from Party City, 800-
727-8924, *partycity.com*. Balloon chandelier kit
from Walmart, *walmart.com*.

FLUTTER BY BUTTERFLY

Photography by John O'Hagan
Styling by Courtni Bodiford
*Recipe Development by Kathleen Kanen and
Vanessa Rocchio • Food Styling by Kathleen Kanen*
Pages 43–58: Royal Albert *Friendship* teapot,
Royal Albert *Gratitude* footed teacup and saucer
set, Royal Albert *Devotion* footed teacup and saucer
set, 3-tiered tray, salad plate, and tidbit plate;
Royal Albert *Bridesmaid* mini creamer, mini open
sugar bowl, and tray; International Silver *Garland*
fork, spoon, and knife from Replacements, Ltd.,
800-737-5223, *replacements.com*. Tablecloth, eyelet
overlay, hemstitch napkins, and teapot spoons
from HomeGoods, 833-888-0776, *homegoods.com*.
Napkin rings from Saro, *sarostore.com*. Butterfly
wings and wands from Amazon, *amazon.com*.

FIT FOR ROYAL-TEA

Photography by John O'Hagan
Styling by Courtni Bodiford
Recipe Development by Janet Lambert
Food Styling by Katie Moon Dickerson
Pages 59–70: Tirschenreuth *Rose* teapot, salad
plate, and two-tiered serving tray; Haviland *The
Princess* flat cup and saucer set, luncheon plate,
butter pat, 12-inch oval serving platter, bread tray,
and 10-inch oval serving platter; Oneida Silver
Brahms demitasse spoon, youth fork, hollow handle
youth knife, and youth spoon from Replacements,
Ltd., 800-737-5223, *replacements.com*. Princess
dresses from HomeGoods, 833-888-0776,
homegoods.com. Tiaras, wardrobe, and princess
dresses from Amazon, *amazon.com*. Buffet from
Hibiscus House, 407-927-6080, *shophibiscushouse
.com*. Location courtesy of Angie Burge.

TIME FOR A FIESTA

Photography by John O'Hagan
Styling by Courtni Bodiford
*Recipe Development by Becca Cummins and
Izzie Turner • Food Styling by Kathleen Kanen*
Pages 71–84: Anfora *Puebla Blue* bread and
butter plate, 12-inch round platter, bowls for
condiments, 12-inch oval platter, and 9-inch oval
platter; Anfora *Puebla Palm Leaf* salad plate from
Replacements, Ltd., 800-737-5223, *replacements
.com*. Homer Laughlin *Fiesta* oval vegetable bowl
in turquoise and fruit salad bowl in poppy from
Belk, 866-235-5443, *belk.com*. Our Table *Maddox
Mirror* salad fork and teaspoon; Our Table *Hollis*
spreader and demitasse spoon from Bed, Bath, &
Beyond, 800-462-3966, *bedbathandbeyond.com*.
Linen for scones, napkins, and striped runner from
World Market, 877-967-5362, *worldmarket.com*.
Yellow tablecloth, floor poufs, and rattan chairs
from HomeGoods, 833-888-0776, *homegoods.com*.
Large piñata, mini piñatas, sombreros, maracas,
streamers, and garland from Amazon, *amazon
.com*. Succulents and plant pots from Trader Joe's,
traderjoes.com. Vintage Homer Laughlin *Fiesta*
teapot and other dishes from private collection.

TEA WITH FOREST FRIENDS

Photography by John O'Hagan
Styling by Courtni Bodiford
*Recipe Development and Food Styling by
Kathleen Kanen*
Pages 85–96: Magic Cabin *Woodland Friends* tea
set from *ebay.com*. Metlox *Lotus* Lime Green salad
plate; Oneida *Silver Chateau* 3-piece youth set;

Pottery Barn China *Harvest Leaf* salad plate from
Replacements, Ltd., 800-737-5223, *replacements
.com*. Wood slice pedestal stand from World Market,
877-967-5362, *worldmarket.com*. April Cornell
Mums tablecloth from April Cornell, 888-332-7745,
aprilcornell.com. Hearth & Hand napkins from
Target, 800-591-3869, *target.com*.

AFTERNOON TEA FOR MERMAIDS

Photography by John O'Hagan
Styling by Courtni Bodiford
Recipe Development by Laura Crandall
Food Styling by Katie Moon Dickerson
Pages 97–110: Blue Sky *Seawave Turquoise Blue*
teapot, creamer, covered sugar bowl, and 8-inch
shell shaped dish; Blue Sky *Seawave White* flat
cup and saucer set; Blue Sky *Seahorse and Seashell
Menagerie Blue* salad plate, figural appetizer plate,
sauce dish, spreader, 14-inch figural serving bowl,
and 12-inch rectangular tray; Blue Sky *Seahorse and
Seashell Menagerie White* 14-inch figural platter,
11-inch figural serving bowl, 12-inch rectangular
tray, and salad plates; Reed & Barton *1800* salad
fork and teaspoon; Oneida Silver *Classic Shell*
demitasse spoon from Replacements, Ltd., 800-
737-5223, *replacements.com*. Cake stand from
Williams Sonoma, 877-812-6235, *williams-sonoma
.com*. Blue tablecloth from HomeGoods, 833-
888-0776, *homegoods.com*. Linen for scones bowl
from Colordrift, 718-422-0140, *colordrift.com*.
Napkins from Hen House Linens, 334-625-0391,
henhouselinens.com. Mermaid wallpaper and balloon
arch kit from Amazon, *amazon.com*.

RAINBOWS & UNICORNS

Photography by John O'Hagan
Styling by Courtni Bodiford
Recipe Development by Janet Lambert
Food Styling by Vanessa Rocchio
Pages 111–122: Grace's Teaware *Pink Rose Dots*
teapot and warmer stand, creamer, covered sugar
bowl, salad plate, footed cup and saucer set, pink
footed cup and saucer set, 2-tiered serving tray;
Reed and Barton *Dresden Rose* flat handle butter
spreader, salad fork and teaspoon; Lenox *Carousel
Animals* carousel unicorn from Replacements, Ltd.,
800-737-5223, *replacements.com*. Star and rainbow
wall decals and unicorn headbands from Amazon,
amazon.com. Pink tablecloth from H&M, 855-466-
7467, *www2.hm.com*.

BACK COVER

Photography by John O'Hagan
Styling by Courtni Bodiford
Recipe Development by Izzie Turner
Food Styling by Kathleen Kanen
Zealax *Ballet* teapot from Amazon, *amazon.com*.
Ceralene *Romantique* handled cake plate from
Replacements, Ltd., 800-737-5223, *replacements
.com*. White tablecloth from Sferra, 732-225-6290,
sferra.com.

*EDITOR'S NOTE: Items not listed are from private
collections, and no manufacturer/pattern information
is available.*

Recipe Index

EDITOR'S NOTE: *Recipe titles shown in gold are gluten-free, provided gluten-free versions of processed ingredients (such as flours and extracts) are used.*